I AM THE DARKER BROTHER

AN ANTHOLOGY OF MODERN POEMS
BY AFRICAN AMERICANS

REVISED EDITION

*Edited and with an afterword
by Arnold Adoff*

Drawings by Benny Andrews

Introduction by Rudine Sims Bishop

Foreword by Nikki Giovanni

ALADDIN PAPERBACKS

25 Years of Magical Reading

ALADDIN PAPERBACKS
EST. 1972

First Aladdin Paperbacks edition January 1997
Copyright © 1997 by ALADDIN PAPERBACKS. An imprint of Simon & Schuster Children's Publishing Division, 1230 Avenue of the Americas, New York, NY 10020. All rights reserved, including the right of reproduction in whole or in part in any form. Also available in a Simon & Schuster Books for Young Readers edition. The text of this book was set in 9-point Garamond 3 bold. Printed and bound in the United States of America.   10 9 8 7 6 5 4 3 2

Library of Congress Cataloging-in-Publication Data
I am the darker brother : an anthology of modern poems by African Americans / edited and with an afterword by Arnold Adoff ; drawings by Benny Andrews ; intro. by Rudine Sims Bishop ; preface by Nikki Giovanni. —Rev. ed.
p.   cm.
ISBN 0-689-80869-0 (ps).
1. American poetry—Afro-American authors.   2. American poetry—20th century.
3. Afro-Americans—Poetry. I. Adoff, Arnold. II.. Andrews, Benny, 1930–
PS591.N4I3   1997
811'.5080896073—dc20   96-31242   CIP

Thanks are given to the following for permission to include copyrighted selections: W.W. Norton & Company, Inc., for "Endangered Species," from *Greed* by AI. Copyright © 1993 by AI. Samuel Allen (Paul Vesey) for his "If the Stars Should Fall," "A Moment Please," and "American Gothic." Random House, Inc., for "Our Grandmothers," from *I Shall Not Be Moved* by Maya Angelou. Copyright © 1990 by Maya Angelou. The Sterling Lord Literistic Agency for "Ka'Ba," "Each Morning" by Amiri Baraka, copyright © 1965 by Amiri Baraka, from *New Negro Poets* (Indiana U. Press), and "A Poem for Black Hearts" by Amiri Baraka, copyright © 1965 by Amiri Baraka, from *Negro Digest* (September 1965). Arna Bontemps for his "A Black Man Talks of Reaping," "Southern Mansion," and "The Daybreakers" from *American Negro Poetry* (Hill & Wang), edited by Arna Bontemps. Gwendolyn Brooks for her "Martin Luther King, Jr." Harper & Row, Publishers, for "Bonzeville Man with a Belt in the Back," copyright © 1960 by Gwendolyn Brooks Blakely; "We Real Cool," copyright © 1959 by Gwendolyn Brooks Blakely and "A Song in the Front Yard," copyright 1945 by Gwendolyn Brooks Blakely; from *Selected Poems* by Gwendolyn Brooks. Sterling A. Brown for his "Old Lem." Lucille Clifton for her "listen children." "listen children" copyright © 1987 by Lucille Clifton. Reprinted from *Good Woman: Poems and a Memoir 1969–1980* by Lucille Clifton, with permission of BOA Editions, Ltd., 260 East Ave., Rochester NY 14604. Beacon Press for "Montgomery," copyright © 1968, 1969, 1970, 1971 by Sam Cornish from *Generations* by Sam Cornish. Harper & Row, Publishers, for "Incident"; "For a Lady I Know"; "Yet Do I Marvel," copyright 1925 by Harper & Brothers, renewed 1953 by Ida M. Cullen and "From the Dark Tower," copyright 1927 by Harper & Brothers, renewed 1955 by Ida M. Cullen; from *On These I Stand* by Countee Cullen. Frank Marshall Davis for his "Flowers of Darkness." University of Pittsburgh Press

FOR LEIGH AND JAIME IN HONOR OF THEIR GRANDPARENTS: KENNETH JAMES HAMILTON, ETTA BELLE PERRY HAMILTON, AARON JACOB ADOFF, AND REBECCA STEIN ADOFF

CONTENTS

GENEALOGY

SHALL BE REMEMBERED

IF WE MUST DIE

I AM THE DARKER BROTHER

THE HOPE OF YOUR UNBORN

Introduction:
NOTES FROM A DARKER SISTER

The first edition of *I Am the Darker Brother* appeared in 1968, a time when few Black writers were being published, and virtually no comprehensive anthologies of Black poetry were available to young people. Five years earlier, in 1963, Arna Bontemps had edited *American Negro Poetry,* an anthology that included many of the same poets as *I Am the Darker Brother,* but a selection of poems pitched for an adult audience. Bontemps' anthology of poems for children, *Golden Slippers,* had been published in 1941. Nor were many Black poets producing poems specifically for young people. It had been eleven years since the publication of Gwendolyn Brooks' *Bronzeville Boys and Girls,* and thirty-six years since Langston Hughes' *The Dream Keeper,* a collection of his poems chosen for a young audience. In 1968, Eloise Greenfield had not yet had a book published, and Nikki Giovanni's *Spin a Soft Black Song* and *Ego-tripping,* her first collections for young people, would not arrive until the early seventies. *I Am the Darker Brother,* then, was an extraordinary and timely gift to young American readers.

I thought it was also a gift to me, personally. I became acquainted with the anthology as a graduate student and instructor-intern at Wayne State University in Detroit where, beginning in 1969, I taught undergraduate courses in children's literature, using books from the teaching collection of the Children's Literature Center, one sub-section of which, the "Darker Brother Collection," contained a small but growing selection of books by and about African Americans. This anthology was a focal point of the collection, and it was a revelation to me, an African American doctoral student, whose literary education in racially integrated, but overwhelmingly white, small-town Northern schools, had focused mainly on the typical "dead white male" canon. Yes, I knew some of Langston Hughes' works, and my mother had recited Paul Laurence Dunbar when I was a child. I was vaguely aware of Gwendolyn Brooks, and I had often read James Weldon Johnson's "The Creation" to my third-graders when I was an elementary school teacher. But many of the poets whose work appeared in *I Am the Darker Brother* were, sad to say, strangers to me, and I am indebted to Arnold Adoff for my introduction to them.

In compiling his collection, Arnold had taken action to prevent other young Americans from growing up in ignorance of an important aspect of their literary heritage. He had been teaching in Harlem and on the upper West Side of

New York since 1957. Having discovered that standard textbook literature anthologies included few, if any, works by Black Americans, or works that seemed relevant to the Black, Hispanic, and White urban youngsters whom he was teaching, he started gathering poems by Black poets for use with his students. By the late 1960s, he had accumulated an impressive collection, which became the foundation for *I Am the Darker Brother*. It was Adoff's first book, and he has since become one of the most highly respected poets and anthologists in the field of children's and young adult literature.

In publishing an anthology of Black poetry, Adoff called attention to the regrettable neglect of this element of American literature in schools. In selecting the poems and poets, he called attention to voices that had essentially been suppressed in school curricula, and he subtly challenged American schools to live up to their democratic promise. The very production of this anthology, then, was in some sense a political act, in keeping with the activist and non-conformist stances Adoff had been taking since he was a teenager. He had managed, for instance, to graduate from a high school that specialized in science and mathematics having mostly avoided those subjects to focus on history, English, and music. At City College, he was president of the student chapter of the Americans for Democratic Action, a group that supports liberal political causes. He picketed to integrate lunch counters in Baltimore in 1953, well before the famous student sit-ins of the 1960s. It was fitting then, that this young Jewish poet, committed to social justice, would be in the vanguard of those working to expand the horizons of the field of children's literature. To this day, it is likely that he has published more anthologies of Black American poetry for a wide range of readers—from young children to adults—than any other single individual.

For readers unfamiliar with African American literature, this anthology was a splendid introduction. The list of the thirty poets whose work is included in the first edition of *I Am the Darker Brother* reads like a "who's who" of modern Black American literature: Paul Laurence Dunbar, James Weldon Johnson, Langston Hughes, Claude McKay, Countee Cullen, Jean Toomer, Arna Bontemps, Gwendolyn Brooks, LeRoi Jones (now Amiri Baraka), Margaret Walker, Richard Wright. A few, such as Dunbar, had been born in the late 19th century; many were part of the famous Harlem Renaissance of the 1920s; and several were, at the time of the first edition, among the younger poets of the day.

The poems, grouped thematically, offer a dramatic and provocative vision of what it means to be a Black American. They affirm some of the ways we see ourselves, plumb our ancestry and roots, recount some of the wrongs that have been visited upon us, celebrate some of our heroes, challenge American racism, and express some of our hopes and dreams. They were not written especially for a juvenile audience, but are accessible, even if sometimes challenging. They are often strongly emotional, and they disallow complacency. Together they offer a glimpse into both the unity and the diversity of the Black experience in this nation.

In the nearly thirty years since the first edition of *I Am the Darker Brother,* much has changed in the field of children's and young adult literature, although much has remained the same. In the 1990s, poetry is receiving considerably more attention in classrooms and in juvenile publishing than it did in the 1960s. Collections of poetry are, as a result, much more plentiful. Multiculturalism is a current concern, and literature by and about people is much more in vogue than it was in 1968. A few more Black poets are writing especially for young people. Still, *I Am the Darker Brother* remains a classic, in that it introduces its readers to poets and poems that offer a representative sampling of the canon of American Black poetry. It has lost none of its timeliness.

This second edition includes twenty-one new poems, the work of nineteen additional poets, including nine women. Among the best known of the added poets are Rita Dove, Nikki Giovanni, Maya Angelou, Alice Walker, Audre Lorde, Lucille Clifton, and Ishmael Reed. These are mainly younger, more contemporary poets than those of the first edition, but their poems echo the same themes, confirming the power of those themes to capture the re-curring and ongoing concerns of Black poets and writers.

This second edition of *I Am the Darker Brother* is an excellent gift to a new generation of young readers. If these poems illuminate the Black experience in America, they also place that experience in the context of American literature and social history. They are reminders, in this era of controversies over multiculturalism and affirmative action, that the song of America, which invariably includes some dissonance, requires a multi-voiced chorus; and that, as Langston Hughes notes in the title poem, the 'darker brother' (and, I would like to add, the darker sister) sings America, too.

RUDINE SIMS BISHOP
The Ohio State University
July, 1996

Foreword:
THE POEM SPEAKS

At some point you get tired of being perceived as a problem. You get tired of asking people to treat you fairly. You get tired of petitioning the powers that be for the right to have dreams and the sufficiency to work toward their fulfillment. You turn to poetry in those moments.

Our ancestors wondered who would tell their story. Denied the ability to read and write, forbidden to husband knowledge for their future, punished for sharing knowledge of their past, they turned to poems to shoulder the burden of a voice to the voiceless; hope to the hopeless; prayer to the Godforsaken. They looked to poems for a proper response.

And poetry did not let them down. Poems shouted the truth; mumbled the pain; threatened with anger;

soothed with love. Poems lifted our spirits, shared our joy; accepted our burdens, expressed our shame. And poems are with us still. To light the paths; to close painful doors; to embrace the possible; to dream the improbable.

Sometimes you really just get tired of being a problem. And we turn to poems for an affirmation of our spirits. I Am, indeed, The Darker Brother. I will sit at the table. I will grow and be strong. Tell them, poem, who we are. We, too, are America.

NIKKI GIOVANNI

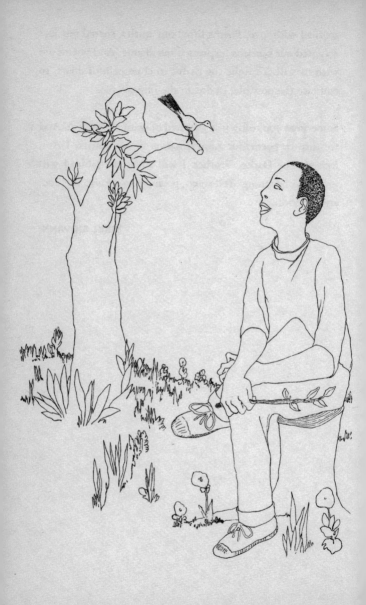

LIKE I AM

ME AND THE MULE

Langston Hughes

My old mule,
He's got a grin on his face.
He's been a mule for so long
He's forgot about his race.

I'm like that old mule —
Black — and don't give a damn!
You got to take me
Like I am.

THE REBEL

MARI EVANS

When I
die
I'm sure
I will have a
Big Funeral . . .
Curiosity
seekers . . .
coming to see
if I
am really
Dead . . .
or just
trying to make
Trouble . . .

WE REAL COOL

GWENDOLYN BROOKS

The Pool Players
Seven At the Golden Shovel

We real cool. We
Left school. We

Lurk late. We
Strike straight. We

Sing sin. We
Thin gin. We

Jazz June. We
Die soon.

CROSS

LANGSTON HUGHES

My old man's a white old man
And my old mother's black.
If ever I cursed my white old man
I take my curses back.

If ever I cursed my black old mother
And wished she were in hell,
I'm sorry for that evil wish
And now I wish her well.

My old man died in a fine big house.
My ma died in a shack.
I wonder where I'm gonna die,
Being neither white nor black?

AUNT JANE ALLEN

FENTON JOHNSON

State Street is lonely today. Aunt Jane Allen has driven
her chariot to Heaven.

I remember how she hobbled along, a little woman,
parched of skin, brown as the leather of a satchel
and with eyes that scanned eighty years of
life.

Have those who bore her dust to the last resting place
buried with her the basket of aprons she went up
and down State Street trying to sell?

Have those who bore her dust to the last resting place
buried with her the gentle word *Son* that she gave
to each of the seed of Ethiopia?

THE WHIPPING

ROBERT HAYDEN

The old woman across the way
    is whipping the boy again
and shouting to the neighborhood
    her goodness and his wrongs.

Wildly he crashes through elephant ears,
    pleads in dusty zinnias,
while she in spite of crippling fat
    pursues and corners him.

She strikes and strikes the shrilly circling
    boy till the stick breaks
in her hand. His tears are rainy weather
    to woundlike memories:

My head gripped in bony vise
    of knees, the writhing struggle
to wrench free, the blows, the fear
    worse than blows that hateful

Words could bring, the face that I
    no longer knew or loved . . .
Well, it is over now, it is over,
    and the boy sobs in his room,

And the woman leans muttering against
a tree, exhausted, purged —
avenged in part for lifelong hidings
she has had to bear.

THOSE WINTER SUNDAYS

ROBERT HAYDEN

Sundays too my father got up early
and put his clothes on in the blueblack cold,
then with cracked hands that ached
from labor in the weekday weather made
banked fires blaze. No one ever thanked him.

I'd wake and hear the cold splintering, breaking.
When the rooms were warm, he'd call,
and slowly I would rise and dress,
fearing the chronic angers of that house,

Speaking indifferently to him,
who had driven out the cold
and polished my good shoes as well.
What did I know, what did I know
of love's austere and lonely offices?

FLASH CARDS

RITA DOVE

In math I was the whiz kid, keeper
of oranges and apples. *What you don't understand,
master,* my father said; the faster
I answered, the faster they came.

I could see one bud on the teacher's geranium,
one clear bee sputtering at the wet pane.
The tulip trees always dragged after heavy rain
so I tucked my head as my boots slapped home.

My father put up his feet after work
and relaxed with a highball and *The Life of Lincoln.*
After supper we drilled and I climbed the dark

before sleep, before a thin voice hissed
numbers as I spun on a wheel. I had to guess.
Ten. I kept saying, *I'm only ten.*

NIKKI-ROSA

Nikki Giovanni

childhood remembrances are always a drag
if you're Black
you always remember things like living in Woodlawn
with no inside toilet
and if you become famous or something
they never talk about how happy you were to have
   your mother
all to yourself and
how good the water felt when you got your bath from
   one of those
big tubs that folk in Chicago barbecue in
and somehow when you talk about home
it never gets across how much you
understood their feelings
as the whole family attended meetings about Hollydale
and even though you remember
your biographers never understand
your father's pain as he sells his stock
   and another dream goes
and though you're poor it isn't poverty that
concerns you
and though they fought a lot
it isn't your father's drinking that makes any difference
but only that everybody is together and you

and your sister have happy birthdays and very good
    Christmasses
and I really hope no white person ever has cause to
    write about me
because they never understand Black love is Black
    wealth and they'll
probably talk about my hard childhood and never
    understand that
all the while I was quite happy

A SONG IN THE FRONT YARD

GWENDOLYN BROOKS

I've stayed in the front yard all my life.
I want a peek at the back
Where it's rough and untended and hungry weed
   grows.
A girl gets sick of a rose.

I want to go in the back yard now
And maybe down the alley,
To where the charity children play.
I want a good time today.

They do some wonderful things.
They have some wonderful fun.
My mother sneers, but I say it's fine
How they don't have to go in at a quarter to nine.
My mother she tells me that Johnnie Mae
Will grow up to be a bad woman.
That George'll be taken to jail soon or late.
(On account of last winter he sold our back gate.)

But I say it's fine. Honest I do.
And I'd like to be a bad woman too,
And wear the brave stockings of night-black lace.
And strut down the streets with paint on my face.

FLOWERS
OF DARKNESS

FRANK MARSHALL DAVIS

Slowly the night blooms, unfurling
Flowers of darkness, covering
The trellised sky, becoming
A bouquet of blackness
Unending
Touched with sprigs
Of pale and budding stars

Soft the night smell
Among April trees
Soft and richly rare
Yet commonplace
Perfume on a cosmic scale

I turn to you Mandy Lou
I see the flowering night
Cameo condensed
Into the lone black rose
Of your face
The young woman-smell
Of your poppy body
Rises to my brain as opium

Yet silently motionless
I sit with twitching fingers
Yea, even reverently
Sit I
With you and the blossoming night
For what flower, plucked,
Lingers long?

JUKE BOX LOVE SONG

LANGSTON HUGHES

I could take the Harlem night
and wrap around you,
Take the neon lights and make a crown,
Take the Lenox Avenue buses,
Taxis, subways,
And for your love song tone their rumble down.
Take Harlem's heartbeat,
Make it a drumbeat,
Put it on a record, let it whirl,
And while we listen to it play,
Dance with you till day —
Dance with you, my sweet brown Harlem girl.

THE GLORY
OF THE DAY WAS
IN HER FACE

JAMES WELDON JOHNSON

The glory of the day was in her face,
The beauty of the night was in her eyes.
And over all her loveliness, the grace
Of Morning blushing in the early skies.

And in her voice, the calling of the dove;
Like music of a sweet, melodious part.
And in her smile, the breaking light of love;
And all the gentle virtues in her heart.

And now the glorious day, the beauteous night,
The birds that signal to their mates at dawn,
To my dull ears, to my tear-blinded sight
Are one with all the dead, since she is gone.

BRONZEVILLE MAN WITH A BELT IN THE BACK

GWENDOLYN BROOKS

In such an armor he may rise and raid
The dark cave after midnight, unafraid,
And slice the shadows with his able sword
Of good broad nonchalance, hashing them down.

And come out and accept the gasping crowd,
Shake off the praises with an airiness.
And, searching, see love shining in an eye,
But never smile.

In such an armor he cannot be slain.

MADHOUSE

CALVIN C. HERNTON

Here is a place that is no place
And here is no place that is a place
A place somewhere beyond the reaches of time
And beyond the reaches of those who in time
Bring flowers and fruit to this place,
Yet here is a definite place
And a definite time, fixed
In a timelessness of precise vantage
From which to view flowers and view fruit
And those who come bearing them.

Those who come by Sunday's habit are weary
And kiss us half-foreign but sympathetic,
Spread and eat noisily to crack the unbearable
Silence of this place:
They do not know that something must always come
From something and that nothing must come always
From nothing, and that nothing is always a thing

To drive us mad.

KA'BA

Amiri Baraka

A closed window looks down
on a dirty courtyard, and black people
call across or scream across or walk across
defying physics in the stream of their will

Our world is full of sound
Our world is more lovely than anyone's
tho we suffer, and kill each other
and sometimes fail to walk the air

We are beautiful people
with african imaginations
full of masks and dances and swelling chants
with african eyes, and noses, and arms,
though we sprawl in gray chains in a place
full of winters, when what we want is sun.

We have been captured,
brothers. And we labor
to make our getaway, into
the ancient image, into a new

correspondence with ourselves
and our black family. We need magic
now we need the spells, to raise up
return, destroy, and create. What will be

the sacred words?

FOR POETS

AL YOUNG

Stay beautiful
but don't stay down underground too long
Don't turn into a mole
or a worm
or a root
or a stone

Come on out into the sunlight
Breathe in trees
Knock out mountains
Commune with snakes
& be the very hero of birds

Don't forget to poke your head up
& blink
think
Walk all around
Swim upstream

Don't forget to fly

GENEALOGY

EACH MORNING

(Section 4 from "Hymn for Lanie Poo")

AMIRI BARAKA

Each morning
I go down
to Gansevoort St.
and stand on the docks.
I stare out
at the horizon
until it gets up
and comes to embrace
me. I
make believe
it is my father.
This is known
as genealogy.

A MOMENT PLEASE

SAMUEL ALLEN (PAUL VESEY)

When I gaze at the sun
    I walked to the subway booth
    for change for a dime.
and know that this great earth
    Two adolescent girls stood there
    alive with eagerness to know
is but a fragment from it thrown
    all in their new found world
    there was for them to know
in heat and flame a billion years ago,
    they looked at me and brightly asked
    "Are you Arabian?"
that then this world was lifeless
    I smiled and cautiously
    — for one grows cautious —
    shook my head.
as, a billion hence,
    "Egyptian?"
it shall again be,
    Again I smiled and shook my head
    and walked away.
what moment is it that I am betrayed,
    I've gone but seven paces now
oppressed, cast down,

and from behind comes swift the sneer
or warm with love or triumph?
    "Or Nigger?"

    A moment, please
What is it that to fury I am roused?
    for still it takes a moment
What meaning for me
    and now
in this homeless clan
    I'll turn
the dupe of space
    and smile
the toy of time?
    and nod my head.

THE NEGRO SPEAKS OF RIVERS

To W.E.B. DuBois

LANGSTON HUGHES

I've known rivers:
I've known rivers ancient as the world and older than
the flow of human blood in human veins.

My soul has grown deep like the rivers.

I bathed in the Euphrates when dawns were young.
I built my hut near the Congo and it lulled me to
sleep.
I looked upon the Nile and raised the pyramids above
it.
I heard the singing of the Mississippi when Abe
Lincoln went down to New Orleans, and I've seen
its muddy bosom turn all golden in the sunset.
I've known rivers:
Ancient, dusky rivers.

My soul has grown deep like the rivers.

SOUTHERN MANSION

Arna Bontemps

Poplars are standing there still as death
And ghosts of dead men
Meet their ladies walking
Two by two beneath the shade
And standing on the marble steps.

There is a sound of music echoing
Through the open door
And in the field there is
Another sound tinkling in the cotton:
Chains of bondmen dragging on the ground.

The years go back with an iron clank,
A hand is on the gate,
A dry leaf trembles on the wall.
Ghosts are walking.
They have broken roses down
And poplars stand there still as death.

O DAEDALUS,
FLY AWAY HOME

ROBERT HAYDEN

Drifting night in the Georgia pines,
coonskin drum and jubilee banjo.
   Pretty Malinda, dance with me.

Night is juba, night is conjo.
   Pretty Malinda, dance with me.

Night is an African juju man
weaving a wish and a weariness together
   to make two wings.

   O fly away home fly away

Do you remember Africa?

   O cleave the air fly away home

My gran, he flew back to Africa,
just spread his arms and
   flew away home.

Drifting night in the windy pines;
night is a laughing, night is a longing.
Pretty Malinda, come to me.

Night is a mourning juju man
weaving a wish and a weariness together
to make two wings.

   O fly away home fly away

OCTOBER JOURNEY

MARGARET WALKER

Traveler take heed for journeys undertaken in the
    dark of the year.
Go in the bright blaze of Autumn's equinox.
Carry protection against ravages of a sun-robber, a
    vandal, and a thief.
Cross no bright expanse of water in the full of the
    moon.
Choose no dangerous summer nights;
no heady tempting hours of spring;
October journeys are safest, brightest, and best.

I want to tell you what hills are like in October
when colors gush down mountainsides
and little streams are freighted with a caravan of
    leaves.
I want to tell you how they blush and turn in fiery
    shame and joy,
how their love burns with flames consuming and
    terrible
until we wake one morning and woods are like a
    smoldering plain —

a glowing caldron full of jeweled fire:
the emerald earth a dragon's eye
the poplars drenched with yellow light
and dogwoods blazing bloody red.

Traveling southward earth changes from gray rock
    to green velvet.
Earth changes to red clay
with green grass growing brightly
with saffron skies of evening setting dully
with muddy rivers moving sluggishly.

In the early spring when the peach tree blooms
wearing a veil like a lavender haze
and the pear and plum in their bridal hair
gently snow their petals on earth's grassy bosom below
then the soughing breeze is soothing
and the world seems bathed in tenderness,
but in October
blossoms have long since fallen.
A few red apples hang on leafless boughs;
wind whips bushes briskly.
And where a blue stream sings cautiously
a barren land feeds hungrily.

An evil moon bleeds drops of death.
The earth burns brown.
Grass shrivels and dries to a yellowish mass.
Earth wears a dun-colored dress
like an old woman wooing the sun to be her lover,
be her sweetheart and her husband bound in one.
Farmers heap hay in stacks and bind corn in shocks
against the biting breath of frost.

The train wheels hum, "I am going home, I am going
   home,
I am moving toward the South."
Soon cypress swamps and muskrat marshes
and black fields touched with cotton will appear.
I dream again of my childhood land
of a neighbor's yard with a redbud tree
the smell of pine for turpentine
an Easter dress, a Christmas eve
and winding roads from the top of a hill.
A music sings within my flesh
I feel the pulse within my throat
my heart fills up with hungry fear
while hills and flatlands stark and staring
before my dark eyes sad and haunting
appear and disappear.

Then when I touch this land again
the promise of a sun-lit hour dies.
The greenness of an apple seems
to dry and rot before my eyes.
The sullen winter rains
are tears of grief I cannot shed.
The windless days are static lives.
The clock runs down
timeless and still.
The days and nights turn hours to years
and water in a gutter marks the circle of another
    world
hating, resentful, and afraid
stagnant, and green, and full of slimy things.

DUST BOWL

ROBERT A. DAVIS

These were our fields.
Now no flower blooms,
No grain grows here
Where earth moves in every wind.

No birds nest in these trees.
No fruit hangs
Where the boughs stretch bare
In the sun.

The dust sifts down — blows in.
Our mouths are filled.
The dust moves across,
And up and around the dust moves

In our waking — our sleeping —
In our dreams.

A BALLAD OF REMEMBRANCE

ROBERT HAYDEN

Quadroon mermaids, Afro angels, black saints
balanced upon the switchblades of that air
and sang. Tight streets unfolding to the eye
like fans of corrosion and elegiac lace
crackled with their singing: Shadow of time. Shadow
    of blood.

Shadow, echoed the Zulu king, dangling
from a cluster of balloons. Blood,
whined the gun-metal priestess, floating
over the courtyard where dead men diced.

What will you have? she inquired, the sallow vendeuse
    of prepared tarnishes and jokes of nacre and
    ormolu,
what but those gleamings, oldrose graces,
manners like scented gloves? Contrived ghosts
rapped to metronome clack of lavalieres.

Contrived illuminations riding a threat
of river, masked Negroes wearing chameleon
satins gaudy now as a fortuneteller's
dream of disaster, lighted the crazy flopping
dance of love and hate among joys, rejections.

Accommodate, muttered the Zulu king,
toad on a throne of glaucous poison jewels.
Love, chimed the saints and the angels and the
    mermaids.
Hate, shrieked the gun-metal priestess
from her spiked bellcollar curved like a fleur-de-lis:

As well have a talon as a finger, a muzzle as a mouth,
as well have a hollow as a heart. And she pinwheeled
away in coruscations of laughter, scattering
those others before her like foil stars.

But, the dance continued — now among metaphorical
doors, coffee cups floating poised
hysterias, decors of illusion; now among
mazurka dolls offering death's-heads
of cocaine roses and real violets.

Then you arrived, meditative, ironic,
richly human; and your presence was shore where I
    rested
released from the hoodoo of that dance, where I spoke
    with my true voice again.

And therefore this is not only a ballad of remembrance
for the down-South arcane city with death
in its jaws like gold teeth and archaic cusswords;
not only a token for the troubled generous friends
held in the fists of that schizoid city like flowers,
but also, Mark Van Doren,
a poem of remembrance, a gift, a souvenir for you.

MIDDLE PASSAGE

ROBERT HAYDEN

I.
Jesús, Estrella, Esperanza, Mercy:

Sails flashing to the wind like weapons,
sharks following the moans the fever and the dying;
horror the corposant and compass rose.

Middle Passage:
voyage through death
to life upon these shores.

"10 April 1800 —
Blacks rebellious. Crew uneasy. Our linguist says
their moaning is a prayer for death,
ours and their own. Some try to starve themselves.
Lost three this morning leaped with crazy laughter
to the waiting sharks, sang as they went under."

Desire, Adventure, Tartar, Ann:

Standing to America, bringing home
black gold, black ivory, black seed.
Deep in the festering hold thy father lies,
of his bones New England pews are made,
those are altar lights that were his eyes.

Jesus Saviour Pilot Me
Over Life's Tempestuous Sea

We pray that Thou wilt grant, O Lord,
safe passage to our vessels bringing
heathen souls onto Thy chastening.

Jesus Saviour

"8 bells. I cannot sleep, for I am sick
with fear, but writing eases fear a little
since still my eyes can see these words take shape
upon the page & so I write, as one
would turn to exorcism. 4 days scudding,
but now the sea is calm again. Misfortune
follows in our wake like sharks (our grinning
tutelary gods). Which one of us
has killed an albatross? A plague among
our blacks — Ophthalmia: blindness — & we
have jettisoned the blind to no avail.
It spreads, the terrifying sickness spreads.
Its claws have scratched sight from the Capt.'s eyes
& there is blindness in the fo'c'sle
& we must sail 3 weeks before we come
to port."

"What port awaits us, Davy Jones'
or home? I've heard of slavers drifting, drifting,
playthings of wind and storm and chance, their
   crews
gone blind, the jungle hatred
crawling up on deck.

Thou Who Walked On Galilee

"Deponent further sayeth *The Bella J*
left the Guinea Coast
with cargo of five hundred blacks and odd
for the barracoons of Florida:

"That there was hardly room 'tween-decks for half
the sweltering cattle stowed spoon-fashion there;
that some went mad of thirst and tore their flesh
and sucked the blood:

"That Crew and Captain lusted with the comeliest
of the savage girls kept naked in the cabins;
that there was one they called The Guinea Rose
and they cast lots and fought to lie with her:

"That when Bo's'n piped all hands, the flames
spreading from starboard already were beyond
control, the negroes howling and their chains
entangled with the flames:

"That the burning blacks could not be reached,
that the Crew abandoned ship,
leaving their shrieking negresses behind,
that the Captain perished drunken with the
wenches:

"Further Deponent sayeth not."

Pilot Oh Pilot Me

 II.

Aye, lad, and I have seen those factories,
Gambia, Rio Pongo, Calabar;
have watched the artful mongos baiting traps
of war wherein the victor and the vanquished

Were caught as prizes for our barracoons.
Have seen the nigger kings whose vanity
and greed turned wild black hides of Fellatah,
Mandingo, Ibo, Kru to gold for us.

And there was one — King Anthracite we named him —
fetish face beneath French parasols
of brass and orange velvet, impudent mouth
whose cups were carven skulls of enemies:

He'd honor us with drum and feast and conjo
and palm-oil-glistening wenches deft in love,
and for tin crowns that shone with paste,
red calico and German-silver trinkets

Would have the drums talk war and send
his warriors to burn the sleeping villages
and kill the sick and old and lead the young
in coffles to our factories.

Twenty years a trader, twenty years,
for there was wealth aplenty to be harvested
from those black fields, and I'd be trading still
but for the fevers melting down my bones.

 III.

Shuttles in the rocking loom of history,
the dark ships move, the dark ships move,
their bright ironical names
like jests of kindness on a murderer's mouth;
plough through thrashing glister toward
fata morgana's lucent melting shore,
weave toward New World littorals that are
mirage and myth and actual shore.

Voyage through death,
    voyage whose chartings are
        unlove.
A charnel stench, effluvium of living death
spreads outward from the hold,
where the living and the dead, the horribly dying,
lie interlocked, lie foul with blood and excrement.

Deep in the festering hold thy father lies,
the corpse of mercy rots with him,
rats eat love's rotten gelid eyes.

But, oh, the living look at you
with human eyes whose suffering accuses you,
whose hatred reaches through the swill of dark
to strike you like a leper's claw.

You cannot stare that hatred down
or chain the fear that stalks the watches
and breathes on you its fetid scorching breath;
cannot kill the deep immortal human wish,
the timeless will.

    "But for the storm that flung up barriers
    of wind and wave, *The Armistad,* señores,
    would have reached the port of Príncipe in two,
    three days at most; but for the storm we should
    have been prepared for what befell.
    Swift as the puma's leap it came. There was

that interval of moonless calm filled only
with the water's and the rigging's usual sounds,
then sudden movement, blows and snarling cries
and they had fallen on us with machete
and marlinspike. It was as though the very
air, the night itself were striking us.
Exhausted by the rigors of the storm,
we were no match for them. Our men went down
before the murderous Africans. Our loyal
Celestino ran from below with gun
and lantern and I saw, before the cane-
knife's wounding flash, Cinquez,
that surly brute who calls himself a prince,
directing, urging on the ghastly work.
He hacked the poor mulatto down, and then
he turned on me. The decks were slippery
when daylight finally came. It sickens me
to think of what I saw, of how these apes
threw overboard the butchered bodies of
our men, true Christians all, like so much jetsam.
Enough, enough. The rest is quickly told:
Cinquez was forced to spare the two of us
you see to steer the ship to Africa,
and we like phantoms doomed to rove the sea
voyaged east by day and west by night,
deceiving them, hoping for rescue,
prisoners on our own vessel, till
at length we drifted to the shores of this
your land, America, where we were freed
from our unspeakable misery. Now we

demand, good sirs, the extradition of
Cinquez and his accomplices to La
Havana. And it distresses us to know
there are so many here who seem inclined
to justify the mutiny of these blacks.
We find it paradoxical indeed
that you whose wealth, whose tree of liberty
are rooted in the labor of your slaves
should suffer the august John Quincy Adams
to speak with so much passion of the right
of chattel slaves to kill their lawful masters
and with his Roman rhetoric weave a hero's
garland for Cinquez. I tell you that
we are determined to return to Cuba
with our slaves and there see justice done.
     Cinquez —
or let us say 'the Prince' — Cinquez shall die."

The deep immortal human wish,
the timeless will:

     Cinquez its deathless primaveral image,
     life that transfigures many lives.

Voyage through death
     to life upon these shores.

THE IDEA
OF ANCESTRY

ETHERIDGE KNIGHT

1

Taped to the wall of my cell are 47 pictures: 47 black
faces: my father, mother, grandmothers (1 dead), grand
fathers (both dead), brothers, sisters, uncles, aunts,
cousins (1st and 2nd), nieces, and nephews. They stare
across the space at me sprawling on my bunk. I know
their dark eyes, they know mine. I know their style,
they know mine. I am all of them, they are all of me;
they are farmers, I am a thief, I am me, they are thee.

I have at one time or another been in love with my
      mother,
1 grandmother, 2 sisters, 2 aunts (1 went to the asylum),
and 5 cousins. I am now in love with a 7 yr old niece
(she sends me letters written in large block print, and her
picture is the only one that smiles at me).

I have the same name as 1 grandfather, 3 cousins, 3
      nephews,
and 1 uncle. The uncle disappeared when he was 15,
      just took
off and caught a freight (they say). He's discussed each
      year

when the family has a reunion, he causes uneasiness in

the clan, he is an empty space. My father's mother, who
    is 93

and who keeps the Family Bible with everybody's birth
    dates

(and death dates) in it, always mentions him. There is
    no

place in her Bible for "whereabouts unknown."

2

Each Fall the graves of my grandfathers call me, the
    brown

hills and red gullies of Mississippi send out their electric

messages, galvanizing my genes. Last yr/like a salmon
    quitting

the cold ocean — leaping and bucking up his
    birthstream/I

hitchhiked my way from L.A. with 16 caps in my
    pocket and a

monkey on my back / and I almost kicked it with the
    kinfolks.

I walked barefooted in my grandmother's backyard/I
    smelled the old

land and the woods/I sipped cornwhiskey from fruit jars
    with the men/

I flirted with the women/I had a ball till the caps ran out

and my habit came down. That night I looked at my
    grandmother

and split/my guts were screaming for junk/but I was
    almost

.ced/I had almost caught up with me.
    ..ne next day in Memphis I cracked a croaker's crib
    for a fix.)

This yr there is a gray stone wall damming my stream,
    and
    when
the falling leaves stir my genes, I pace my cell or flop on
    my bunk
and stare at 47 black faces across the space. I am all of
    them,
they are all of me, I am me, they are thee, and I have
    no sons
to float in the space between.

BLACKBOTTOM

Toi Derricotte

When relatives came from out of town,
we would drive down to Blackbottom,
drive slowly down the congested main streets —
   Beubian and Hastings —
trapped in the mesh of Saturday night.

Freshly escaped, black middle class,
we snickered, and were proud;
the louder the streets, the prouder.
We laughed at the bright clothes of a prostitute,
a man sitting on a curb with a bottle in his hand.
We smelled barbecue cooking in dented washtubs and
   our mouths watered.
As much as we wanted it we couldn't take the chance.

Rhythm and blues came from the windows, the
   throaty voice of a woman
      lost in the bass, in the drums, in the dirty down and
      out, the grind.
"I love to see a funeral, then I know it ain't mine."
We rolled our windows down so that the waves rolled
   over us like blood.
We hoped to pass invisibly, knowing on Monday we
   would return safely

to our jobs, the post office and classroom.
We wanted our sufferings to be offered up as tender
    meat,
and our triumphs to be belted out in raucous song.
We had lost our voice in the suburbs, in Conant
    Gardens, where each
    brick house delineated a fence of silence;
we had lost the right to sing in the street and damn
    creation.

We returned to wash our hands of them,
to smell them
whose very existence
tore us down to the human.

now poem.   for us.

SONIA SANCHEZ

don't let them die out
all these old / blk / people
don't let them cop out
with their memories
of slavery / survival.
                    it is our
heritage.
    u know. part / african.
part / negro.
        part / slave
sit down with em brothas & sistuhs.
                        talk to em. listen to their
tales of victories / woes / sorrows.
                        listen to their blk /
myths.
    record them talken their ago talk
for our tomorrows.
                    ask them bout the songs of
births. the herbs
        that cured
            their aches.   the crazy /
                    niggers blowen
                    some cracker's cool.

the laughter
comen out of tears,
let them tell us of their juju years
    so ours will be that much stronger.

OUR GRANDMOTHERS

Maya Angelou

She lay, skin down on the moist dirt,
the canebrake rustling
with the whispers of leaves, and
loud longing of hounds and
the ransack of hunters crackling the near branches.

She muttered, lifting her head a nod toward freedom,
I shall not, I shall not be moved.

She gathered her babies,
their tears slick as oil on black faces,
their young eyes canvassing mornings of madness.
Momma, is Master going to sell you
from us tomorrow?

Yes.
Unless you keep walking more
and talking less.
Yes.
Unless the keeper of our lives
releases me from all commandments.
Yes.
And your lives,
never mine to live,

will be executed upon the killing floor of innocents.
Unless you match my heart and words,
saying with me,

I shall not be moved.

In Virginia tobacco fields,
leaning into the curve
on Steinway
pianos, along Arkansas roads,
in the red hills of Georgia,
into the palms of her chained hands, she
cried against calamity,
You have tried to destroy me
and though I perish daily,

I shall not be moved.

Her universe, often
summarized into one black body
falling finally from the tree to her feet,
made her cry each time in a new voice.
All my past hastens to defeat,
and strangers claim the glory of my love,
Iniquity has bound me to his bed,

yet, I must not be moved.

She heard the names,
swirling ribbons in the wind of history:
nigger, nigger bitch, heifer,
mammy, property, creature, ape, baboon,
whore, hot tail, thing, it.
She said, But my description cannot
fit your tongue, for
I have a certain way of being in this world
and I shall not, I shall not be moved.

No angel stretched protecting wings
above the heads of her children,
fluttering and urging the winds of reason
into the confusion of their lives.
They sprouted like young weeds,
but she could not shield their growth
from the grinding blades of ignorance, nor
shape them into symbolic topiaries.
She sent them away,
underground, overland, in coaches and
shoeless.
When you learn, teach.
When you get, give.
As for me,

I shall not be moved.

She stood in midocean, seeking dry land.
She searched God's face.
Assured,
she placed her fire of service
on the altar, and though
clothed in the finery of faith,
when she appeared at the temple door,
no sign welcomed
Black Grandmother. Enter here.

Into the crashing sound,
into wickedness, she cried,
No one, no, nor no one million
ones dare deny me God. I go forth
alone, and stand as ten thousand.
The Divine upon my right
impels me to pull forever
at the latch on Freedom's gate.

The Holy Spirit upon my left leads my
feet without ceasing into the camp of the
righteous and into the tents of the free.

These momma faces, lemon-yellow, plum-purple,
honey-brown, have grimaced and twisted
down a pyramid of years.
She is Sheba and Sojourner,
    Harriet and Zora,
    Mary Bethune and Angela,
    Annie to Zenobia.

She stands
before the abortion clinic,
confounded by the lack of choices.
In the Welfare line,
reduced to the pity of handouts.
Ordained in the pulpit, shielded
by the mysteries.
In the operating room,
husbanding life.
In the choir loft,
holding God in her throat.
On lonely street corners,
hawking her body.
In the classroom, loving the
children to understanding.

Centered on the world's stage,
she sings to her loves and beloveds,
to her foes and detractors:
However I am perceived and deceived,
however my ignorance and conceits,
lay aside your fears that I will be undone,

for I shall not be moved.

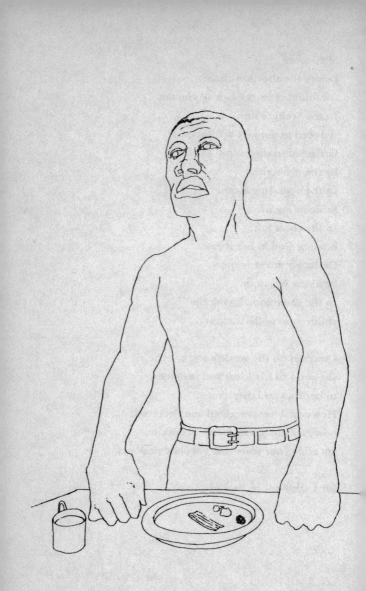

SHALL BE
REMEMBERED

FREDERICK DOUGLASS

ROBERT HAYDEN

When it is finally ours, this freedom, this liberty, this
    beautiful
and terrible thing, needful to man as air,
usable as the earth; when it belongs at last to our
    children,
when it is truly instinct, brainmatter, diastole, systole,
reflex action; when it is finally won; when it is more
than the gaudy mumbo jumbo of politicians:
this man, this Douglass, this former slave, this Negro
beaten to his knees, exiled, visioning a world
where none is lonely, none hunted, alien,
this man, superb in love and logic, this man
shall be remembered — oh, not with statues' rhetoric,
not with legends and poems and wreaths of bronze
    alone,
but with the lives grown out of his life, the lives
fleshing his dream of the needful beautiful thing.

RUNAGATE RUNAGATE

Robert Hayden

I.
Runs falls rises stumbles on from darkness into
    darkness
and the darkness thicketed with shapes of terror
and the hunters pursuing and the hounds pursuing
and the night cold and the night long and the river
to cross and the jack-muh-lanterns beckoning
    beckoning
and blackness ahead and when shall I reach that
    somewhere
morning and keep on going and never turn back
    and keep on going.

Runagate
        Runagate
                Runagate

Many thousands rise and go
many thousands crossing over

O mythic North
O star-shaped yonder Bible city

Some go weeping and some rejoicing
some in coffins and some in carriages
some in silks and some in shackles

    Rise and go fare you well

No more auction block for me
no more driver's lash for me

    If you see my Pompey, 30 yrs of age,
    new breeches, plain stockings, negro shoes;
    if you see my Anna, likely young mulatto
    branded E on the right cheek, R on the left,
    catch them if you can and notify subscriber.
    Catch them if you can, but it won't be easy.
    They'll dart underground when you try to catch
        them,
    plunge into quicksand, whirlpools, mazes,
    turn into scorpions when you try to catch them.

And before I'll be a slave
I'll be buried in my grave

    North star and bonanza gold
    I'm bound for the freedom, freedom-bound
    and oh Susyanna don't you cry for me

        Runagate
            Runagate

II.

Rises from their anguish and their power,
   Harriet Tubman,

   woman of earth, whipscarred,
   a summoning, a shining

   Mean to be free

   And this was the way of it, brethren brethren
   way we journeyed from Can't to Can.
   Moon so bright and no place to hide,
   the cry up and the patterollers riding,
   hound dogs belling in bladed air.
   And fear starts a-murbling, Never make it,
   we'll never make it. *Hush that now,*
   and she's turned upon us, leveled pistol
   glinting in the moonlight:
   Dead folks can't jaybird-talk, she says;
   you keep on going now or die, she says.

Wanted Harriet Tubman alias The General
alias Moses Stealer of Slaves

In league with Garrison Alcott Emerson
Garrett Douglass Thoreau John Brown

Armed and known to be Dangerous

Wanted Reward Dead or Alive

Tell me, Ezekiel, oh tell me do you see
mailed Jehovah coming to deliver me?

Hoot-owl calling in the ghosted air,
five times calling to the hants in the air.
Shadow of a face in the scary leaves,
shadow of a voice in the talking leaves:

Come ride-a my train

Oh that train, ghost-story train
through swamp and savanna movering movering,
over trestles of dew, through caves of the wish,
Midnight Special on a saber track movering movering
first stop Mercy and the last Hallelujah.

Come ride-a my train

Mean mean mean to be free.

MEMORIAL WREATH

(For the more than 200,000 Negroes who served in the Union Army during the Civil War)

DUDLEY RANDALL

In this green month when resurrected flowers,
Like laughing children ignorant of death,
Brighten the couch of those who wake no more,
Love and remembrance blossom in our hearts
For you who bore the extreme sharp pang for us,
And bought our freedom with your lives.

                        And now,
Honoring your memory, with love we bring
These fiery roses, white-hot cotton flowers
And violets bluer than cool northern skies
You dreamed of in the burning prison fields
When liberty was only a faint north star,
Not a bright flower planted by your hands
Reaching up hardy nourished with your blood.

Fit gravefellows you are for Lincoln, Brown
And Douglass and Toussaint . . . all whose rapt eyes
Fashioned a new world in this wilderness.

American earth is richer for your bones;
Our hearts beat prouder for the blood we inherit.

VATICIDE

(For Mohandas Gandhi)

MYRON O'HIGGINS

. . . he is murdered upright in the day
his flesh is opened and displayed. . . .

Into that stricken hour the hunted had gathered.
You spoke . . . some syllable of terror. *Ram!*
They saw it slip from your teeth and dangle, ablaze
Like a diamond on your mouth.
In that perilous place you fell — extinguished.
The instrument, guilt. The act was love

Now they have taken your death to their rooms
And here in this far city a false Spring
Founders in the ruins of your quiet flesh
and deep in your marvelous wounds
The sun burns down
And the seas return to their imagined homes.

A POEM FOR BLACK HEARTS

AMIRI BARAKA

For Malcolm's eyes, when they broke
the face of some dumb white man. For
Malcolm's hands raised to bless us
all black and strong in his image
of ourselves, for Malcolm's words
fire darts, the victor's tireless
thrusts, words hung above the world
change as it may, he said it, and
for this he was killed, for saying,
and feeling, and being/ change, all
collected hot in his heart, For Malcolm's
heart, raising us above our filthy cities,
for his stride, and his beat, and his address
to the grey monsters of the world, For Malcolm's
pleas for your dignity, black men, for your life,
black men, for the filling of your minds
with righteousness, For all of him dead and
gone and vanished from us, and all of him which
clings to our speech black god of our time.
For all of him, and all of yourself, look up,
black man, quit stuttering and shuffling, look up,
black man, quit whining and stooping, for all of him,
For Great Malcolm a prince of the earth,
    let nothing in us rest

until we avenge ourselves for his death, stupid animals that killed him, let us never breathe a pure breath if we fail, and white men call us faggots till the end of the earth.

FOR MALCOLM WHO WALKS IN THE EYES OF OUR CHILDREN

QUINCY TROUPE

He had been coming a very long time,
had been here many times before
in the flesh of other persons
in the spirit of other gods

His eyes had seen flesh turned too stone,
had seen stone turned too flesh
had swam within the minds
of a billion great heroes,

had walked amongst builders
of nations, of the Sphinx, had built
with his own hands those nations,

had come flying across time a cosmic spirit,
an idea, a thought wave transcending
flesh fusion spirit of all centuries,
had come soaring like a sky break

above ominous clouds of sulphur
in a stride so enormous it spanned
the breadth of a peoples bloodshed,

came singing like Coltrane breathing life
into stone statues formed from lies

Malcolm, flaming cosmic spirit who walks
amongst us, we hear your voice
speaking wisdom in the wind,
we see your vision in the life/fires of men,
in our incredible young children
who watch your image
flaming in the sun

TO RICHARD WRIGHT

CONRAD KENT RIVERS

You said that your people
Never knew the full spirit of
Western Civilization.
To be born unnoticed
Is to be born black,
And left out of the grand adventure.

Miseducation, denial,
Are lost in the cruelty of oppression.
And the faint cool kiss of sensuality
Lingers on our cheeks.

The quiet terror brings on silent night.
They are driving us crazy. And our father's
Religion warps his life.

To live day by day
   Is not to live at all.

AMERICAN GOTHIC

To Satch

SAMUEL ALLEN (PAUL VESEY)

Sometimes I feel like I will *never* stop
Just go on forever
'Til one fine mornin'
I'm gonna reach up and grab me a handfulla stars
Swing out my long lean leg
And whip three hot strikes burnin' down the heavens
And look over at God and say
How about that!

WHEN MAHALIA SINGS

QUANDRA PRETTYMAN

We used to gather at the high window
of the holiness church and, on tip-toe,
look in and laugh at the dresses, too small
on the ladies, and how wretched they all
looked — an old garage for a church, for pews,
old wooden chairs. It seemed a lame excuse
for a church. Not solemn or grand,
with no real robed choir, but a loose jazz band,
or so it sounded to our mocking ears.
So we responded to their hymns with jeers.

Sometimes those holiness people would dance,
and this we knew sprang from deep ignorance
of how to rightly worship God, who after
all was pleased not by such foolish laughter
but by the stiffly still hands in our church
where we saw no one jump or shout or lurch
or weep. We laughed to hear those holiness
rhythms making a church a song fest:
we heard this music as the road to sin,
down which they traveled toward that end.

I, since then, have heard the gospel singing
of one who says I worship with clapping
hands and my whole body, God, whom we must
thank for all this richness raised from dust.
Seeing her high-thrown head reminded
me of those holiness high-spirited,
who like angels, like saints, worshiped as whole
men with rhythm, with dance, with singing soul.
Since then, I've learned of my familiar God —
He finds no worship alien or odd.

YARDBIRD'S SKULL

(For Charlie Parker)

OWEN DODSON

The bird is lost,
Dead, with all the music:
Whole sunsets heard the brain's music
Faded to last horizon notes.
I do not know why I hold
This skull, smaller than a walnut's,
Against my ear,
Expecting to hear
The smashed fear
Of childhood from . . . bone;
Expecting to see
Wind nosing red and purple,
Strange gold and magic
On bubbled windowpanes
Of childhood. Shall I hear?
I should hear: this skull
Has been with violets
Not Yorick, or the gravedigger,
Yapping his yelling story,
This skull has been in air,
Sensed his brother, the swallow,
(Its talent for snow and crumbs).
Flown to lost Atlantis islands,

Places of dreaming, swimming, lemmings.
O I shall hear skull skull,
Hear your lame music,
Believe music rejects undertaking,
Limps back.
Remember tiny lasting, we get lonely:
Come sing, come sing, come sing sing
And sing.

MONTGOMERY

(For Rosa Parks)

SAM CORNISH

white woman have you heard
she is too tired to sit in the back
her feet two hundred years old

move to the back or walk
around to the side door how
long can a woman be a cow

your feet will not move
and you never listen
but even if it rains empty

seats will ride through town
i walk for my children
my feet two hundred years old

HERE WHERE COLTRANE IS

MICHAEL S. HARPER

Soul and race
are private dominions,
memories and modal
songs, a tenor blossoming,
which would paint suffering
a clear color but is not in
this Victorian house
without oil in zero degree
weather and a forty-mile-an-hour wind;
it is all a well-knit family:
a love supreme.
Oak leaves pile up on walkway
and steps, catholic as apples
in a special mist of clear white
children who love my children.
I play "Alabama"
on a warped record player
skipping the scratches
on your faces over the fibrous
conical hairs of plastic
under the wooden floors.

Dreaming on a train from New York
to Philly, you hand out six
notes which become an anthem
to our memories of you:
oak, birch, maple,
apple, cocoa, rubber.
For this reason Martin is dead;
for this reason Malcolm is dead;
for this reason Coltrane is dead;
in the eyes of my first son are the browns
of these men and their music.

MARTIN LUTHER KING JR.

GWENDOLYN BROOKS

A man went forth with gifts.

He was a prose poem.
He was a tragic grace.
He was a warm music.

He tried to heal the vivid volcanoes.
His ashes are
    reading the world.

His Dream still wishes to anoint
    the barricades of faith and of control.

His word still burns the center of the sun,
    above the thousands and the
    hundred thousands.

The word was Justice. It was spoken.

So it shall be spoken.
So it shall be done.

IF WE
MUST DIE

IF WE MUST DIE

CLAUDE MCKAY

If we must die — let it not be like hogs
Hunted and penned in an inglorious spot,
While round us bark the mad and hungry dogs,
Making their mock at our accursed lot.
If we must die — oh, let us nobly die,
So that our precious blood may not be shed
In vain; then even the monsters we defy
Shall be constrained to honor us though dead!
Oh, Kinsmen! We must meet the common foe;
Though far outnumbered, let us show us brave,
And for their thousand blows deal one deathblow!
What though before us lies the open grave?
Like men we'll face the murderous, cowardly pack,
Pressed to the wall, dying, but fighting back!

THE LYNCHING

CLAUDE McKAY

His spirit in smoke ascended to high heaven.
His father, by the cruelest way of pain,
Had bidden him to his bosom once again;
The awful sin remained still unforgiven.
All night a bright and solitary star
(Perchance the one that ever guided him,
Yet gave him up at last to Fate's wild whim)
Hung pitifully o'er the swinging char.
Day dawned, and soon the mixed crowds came to view
The ghastly body swaying in the sun:
The women thronged to look, but never a one
Showed sorrow in her eyes of steely blue;
And little lads, lynchers that were to be,
Danced round the dreadful thing in fiendish glee.

"SO QUIETLY"

LESLIE PINCKNEY HILL

News item from The New York Times *on the lynching of a Negro at Smithville, Ga., December 21, 1919: "The train was boarded so quietly . . . that members of the train crew did not know that the mob had seized the Negro until informed by the prisoner's guard after the train had left the town . . . A coroner's inquest held immediately returned the verdict that West came to his death at the hands of unidentified men."*

So quietly they stole upon their prey
And dragged him out to death, so without flaw
Their black design, that they to whom the law
Gave him in keeping, in the broad, bright day,
Were not aware when he was snatched away;
And when the people, with a shrinking awe,
The horror of that mangled body saw,
"By unknown hands!" was all that they could say.

So, too, my country, stealeth on apace
The soul-blight of a nation. Not with drums
Or trumpet blare is that corruption sown,
But quietly — now in the open face
Of day, now in the dark — and when it comes,
Stern truth will never write. "By hands unknown."

THE DAYBREAKERS

ARNA BONTEMPS

We are not come to wage a strife
    With swords upon this hill:
It is not wise to waste the life
    Against a stubborn will.
Yet would we die as some have done:
Beating a way for the rising sun.

SONG FOR
A DARK GIRL

LANGSTON HUGHES

Way Down South in Dixie
   (Break the heart of me)
They hung my dark young lover
   In a cross roads tree.

Way Down South in Dixie
   (Bruised body high in air)
I asked the white Lord Jesus
   What was the use of prayer.

Way Down South in Dixie
   (Break the heart of me)
Love is a naked shadow
   On a gnarled and naked tree.

OLD LEM

STERLING A. BROWN

I talked to old Lem
And old Lem said:
   "They weigh the cotton
   They store the corn
      We only good enough
      To work the rows;
   They run the commissary
   They keep the books
      We gotta be grateful
      For being cheated;
Whippersnapper clerks
Call us out of our name
      We got to say mister
      To spindling boys
They make our figgers
Turn somersets
We buck in the middle
      Say, 'Thankyuh, sah.'
         They don't come by ones
         They don't come by twos
         But they come by tens.
"Their fists stay closed
Their eyes look straight
    Our hands stay open
    Our eyes must fall
       They don't come by ones

They got the manhood
They got the courage
> *They don't come by twos*
>> We got to slink around,
>> Hangtailed hounds.
They burn us when we dogs
They burn us when we men
> *They come by tens. . . .*

"I had a buddy
Six foot of man
Muscled up perfect
Game to the heart
> *They don't come by ones*
Outworked and outfought
Any man or two men
> *They don't come by twos*
He spoke out of turn
At the commissary
They gave him a day
To git out the county.
He didn't take it.
He said 'Come and get me.'
They came and got him.
> *And they came by tens.*
He stayed in the county —
He lays there dead.

> *They don't come by ones*
> *They don't come by twos*
> *But they come by tens.*"

BETWEEN THE WORLD AND ME

RICHARD WRIGHT

And one morning while in the woods I stumbled
    suddenly upon the thing,
Stumbled upon it in a grassy clearing guarded by scaly
    oaks and elms.
And the sooty details of the scene rose, thrusting
    themselves between the world and me. . . .

There was a design of white bones slumbering
    forgottenly upon a cushion of ashes.
There was a charred stump of a sapling pointing a blunt
    finger accusingly at the sky.
There were torn tree limbs, tiny veins of burnt leaves,
    and a scorched coil of greasy hemp;
A vacant shoe, an empty tie, a ripped shirt, a lonely hat,
    and a pair of trousers stiff with black blood.
And upon the tramped grass were buttons, dead
    matches, butt-ends of cigars and cigarettes, peanut
    shells, a drained gin-flask, and a whore's lipstick;
Scattered traces of tar, restless arrays of feathers, and the
    lingering smell of gasoline.
And through the morning air the sun poured yellow sur-
    prise into the eye sockets of a stony skull. . . .
And while I stood my mind was frozen with a cold pity
    for the life that was gone.

The ground gripped my feet and my heart was circled
by icy walls of fear —

The sun died in the sky; a night wind muttered in the
grass and fumbled the leaves in the trees; the
woods poured forth the hungry yelping of hounds;
the darkness screamed with thirsty voices; and the
witnesses rose and lived:

The dry bones stirred, rattled, lifted, melting themselves
into my bones.

The grey ashes formed flesh firm and black, entering
into my flesh.

The gin-flask passed from mouth to mouth; cigars and
cigarettes glowed, the whore smeared the lipstick
red upon her lips,

And a thousand faces swirled around me, clamoring that
my life be burned. . . .

And then they had me, stripped me, battering my teeth
into my throat till I swallowed my own blood.

My voice was drowned in the roar of their voices, and
my black wet body slipped and rolled in their
hands as they bound me to the sapling.

And my skin clung to the bubbling hot tar, falling from
me in limp patches.

And the down and quills of the white feathers sank
into my raw flesh, and I moaned in my agony.

Then my blood was cooled mercifully, cooled by a
baptism of gasoline.

And in a blaze of red I leaped to the sky as pain rose

like water, boiling my limbs.
Panting, begging I clutched childlike, clutched to the
hot sides of death.
Now I am dry bones and my face a stony skull staring
in yellow surprise at the sun. . . .

WHEN I KNOW THE POWER OF MY BLACK HAND

LANCE JEFFERS

I do not know the power of my hand,
I do not know the power of my black hand.

I sit slumped in the conviction that I am powerless,
tolerate ceilings that make me bend.
My godly mind stoops, my ambition is crippled;
I do not know the power of my hand.

I see my children stunted,
my young men slaughtered,
I do not know the mighty power of my hand.

I see the power over my life and death in
another man's hands, and sometimes
I shake my woolly head and wonder:

Lord have mercy! What would it be like . . . to be free?

But when I know the mighty power of my black hand
   I will snatch my freedom from the tyrant's mouth,
know the first taste of freedom on my eager tongue,
sing the miracle of freedom with all the force
   of my lungs,

christen my black land with exuberant creation,
stand independent in the hall of nations,
root submission and dependence from the soil of my soul
and pitch the monument of slavery from my back when
I know the mighty power of my hand!

LYNCHING AND BURNING

PRIMUS ST. JOHN

Men lean toward the wood.
Hoods crease
Until they find people
Where there used to be hoods.
Instead of a story,
The whole thing becomes a scream
    then time, place, far,
    late in the country,
    alone,
    an old man's farm.
Children we used to call charcoal,
Now they smell that way — deliberately,
And the moon stares at smoke like iced tea.

Daughter,
    Once there was a place we called the earth.
    People lived there. Now we live there . . .

ENDANGERED SPECIES

AI

The color of violence is black.
Those are the facts, spreadeagled
against a white background,
where policemen have cornered the enemy,
where he shouldn't be, which is seen.
Of course, they can't always believe their eyes,
so they have to rely on instinct,
which tells them I am incapable
of civilized behavior,
therefore, I am guilty
of driving through my own neighborhood
and must take my punishment
must relax and enjoy
like a good boy.
If not, they are prepared to purge me
of my illusions of justice, of truth,
which is indeed elusive,
much like Sasquatch,
whose footprints and shit
are only the physical evidence
of what cannot be proved to exist,
much like me,
the "distinguished" professor of lit,
pulled from my car,
because I look suspicious.

My briefcase, filled with today's assignment
could contain drugs,
instead of essays arranged
according to quality of content,
not my students' color of skin,
but then who am I to say
that doesn't require a beating too? —
a solution that leaves no confusion
as to who can do whatever he wants to whom,
because there is a line directly
from slave to perpetrator,
to my face staring out of newspapers and TV,
or described over and over as a black male.
I am deprived of my separate identity
and must always be a race instead of a man
going to work in the land of opportunity,
because slavery didn't really disappear.
It simply put on a new mask
and now it feeds off fear
that is mostly justified,
because the suicides of the ghetto
have chosen to take somebody with them
and it may as well be you
passing through fire,
as I'm being taught
that injustice is merely another way
of looking at the truth.

At some point, we will meet
at the tip of the bullet,
the blade, or the whip
as it draws blood,
but only one of us will change,
only one of us will slip
past the captain and crew of this ship
and the other submit to the chains
of a nation
that delivered rhetoric
in exchange for its promises.

I AM
THE DARKER
BROTHER

I, TOO, SING AMERICA

LANGSTON HUGHES

I, too, sing America.

I am the darker brother.
They send me to eat in the kitchen
When company comes,
But I laugh,
And eat well,
And grow strong.

Tomorrow,
I'll be at the table
When company comes.
Nobody'll dare
Say to me,
"Eat in the kitchen,"
Then.

Besides,
They'll see how beautiful I am
And be ashamed —

I, too, am America.

A BLACK MAN TALKS OF REAPING

ARNA BONTEMPS

I have sown beside all waters in my day.
I planted deep, within my heart the fear
That wind or fowl would take the grain away.
I planted safe against this stark, lean year.

I scattered seed enough to plant the land
In rows from Canada to Mexico
But for my reaping only what the hand
Can hold at once is all that I can show.

Yet what I sowed and what the orchard yields
My brother's sons are gathering stalk and root,
Small wonder then my children glean in fields
They have not sown, and feed on bitter fruit.

FROM THE DARK TOWER

COUNTEE CULLEN

We shall not always plant while others reap
The golden increment of bursting fruit,
Not always countenance, abject and mute,
That lesser men should hold their brothers cheap;
Not everlastingly while others sleep
Shall we beguile their limbs with mellow flute,
Not always bend to some more subtle brute;
We were not made eternally to weep.

The night whose sable breast relieves the stark,
White stars is no less lovely being dark,
And there are buds that cannot bloom at all
In light, but crumble, piteous, and fall;
So in the dark we hide the heart that bleeds,
And wait, and tend our agonizing seeds.

ON PASSING TWO NEGROES ON A DARK COUNTRY ROAD SOMEWHERE IN GEORGIA

CONRAD KENT RIVERS

This road is like a tomb
Carrying souls to stranger realms.
A broken face, patched pants, moonlight,
Late dinner and sleep in a crowded room.
Let us hope that our gods dance
And eat cornbread from a wooden spoon,
When night enters
With a cool breeze
To soothe an aching back.

BEEHIVE

Jean Toomer

Within this black hive to-night
There swarm a million bees;
Bees passing in and out the moon,
Bees escaping out the moon,
Bees returning through the moon,
Silver bees intently buzzing,
Silver honey dripping from the swarm of bees
Earth is a waxen cell of the world comb,
And I, a drone,
Lying on my back,
Lipping honey,
Getting drunk with silver honey,
Wish that I might fly out past the moon
And curl forever in some far-off farmyard flower.

TIRED

FENTON JOHNSON

I am tired of work; I am tired of building up somebody
else's civilization.

Let us take a rest, M'Lissy Jane.

I will go down to the Last Chance Saloon, drink a gallon
or two of gin, shoot a game or two of dice, and
sleep the rest of the night on one of Mike's barrels.

You will let the old shanty go to rot, the white people's
clothes turn to dust, and the Calvary Baptist
Church sink to the bottomless pit.

You will spend your days forgetting you married me
and your nights hunting the warm gin Mike serves
the ladies in the rear of the Last Chance Saloon.

Throw the children into the river; civilization has given
us too many. It is better to die than to grow up
and find that you are colored.

Pluck the stars out of the heavens. The stars mark our
destiny. The stars marked my destiny.

I am tired of civilization.

SYMPATHY

PAUL LAURENCE DUNBAR

I know what the caged bird feels, alas!
When the sun is bright on the upland slopes;
When the wind stirs soft through the springing grass
And the river flows like a stream of glass;
When the first bird sings and the first bud opes,
And the faint perfume from its chalice steals —
I know what the caged bird feels!

I know why he beats his wing!
Till its blood is red on the cruel bars;
For he must fly back to his perch and cling
When he fain would be on the bough a-swing;
And a pain still throbs in the old, old scars
And they pulse again with a keener sting —
I know why he beats his wing!

I know why the caged bird sings, ah me,
When his wing is bruised and his bosom sore,
When he beats his bars and would be free;
It is not a carol of joy or glee,
But a prayer that he sends from his heart's deep core,
But a plea, that upward to Heaven he flings —
I know why the caged bird sings!

SORROW IS THE
ONLY FAITHFUL ONE

OWEN DODSON

Sorrow is the only faithful one:
The lone companion clinging like a season
To its original skin no matter what the variations.

If all the mountains paraded
Eating the valleys as they went
And the sun were a cliffure on the highest peak,

Sorrow would be there between
The sparkling and the giant laughter
Of the enemy when the clouds come down to swim.

But I am less, unmagic, black,
Sorrow clings to me more than to doomsday
    mountains
Or erosion scars on a palisade.

Sorrow has a song like a leech
Crying because the sand's blood is dry
And the stars reflected in the lake

Are water for all their twinkling
And bloodless for all their charm.
I have blood, and a song.
SORROW IS THE ONLY FAITHFUL ONE.

IF THE STARS SHOULD FALL

SAMUEL ALLEN (PAUL VESEY)

Again the day
The low bleak day of the stricken years
And now the years.

The huge slow grief drives on
And I wonder why
And I grow cold
And care less
And less and less I care.

If the stars should fall,
I grant them privilege;
Or if the stars should rise to a brighter flame
The mighty dog, the buckled Orion
To excellent purposes appear to gain —
I should renew their privilege
To fall down.

It is all to me the same
The same to me
I say the great Gods, all of them,
All — cold, pitiless —
Let them fall down
Let them buckle and drop.

FOR A LADY I KNOW

COUNTEE CULLEN

She even thinks that up in heaven
Her class lies late and snores,
While poor black cherubs rise at seven
To do celestial chores.

INCIDENT

COUNTEE CULLEN

Once riding in old Baltimore,
   Heart-filled, head-filled with glee,
I saw a Baltimorean
   Keep looking straight at me.

Now I was eight and very small,
   And he was no whit bigger,
And so I smiled, but he poked out
   His tongue, and called me, "Nigger."

I saw the whole of Baltimore
   From May until December;
Of all the things that happened there
   That's all that I remember.

WE WEAR THE MASK

PAUL LAURENCE DUNBAR

We wear the mask that grins and lies,
It hides our cheeks and shades our eyes —
This debt we pay to human guile;
With torn and bleeding hearts we smile,
And mouth with myriad subtleties.

Why should the world be overwise,
In counting all our tears and sighs?
Nay, let them only see us, while
    We wear the mask.

We smile, but, O great Christ, our cries
To thee from tortured souls arise.
We sing, but oh the clay is vile
Beneath our feet, and long the mile;
But let the world dream otherwise,
    We wear the mask!

HOKKU: IN THE FALLING SNOW

RICHARD WRIGHT

In the falling snow
A laughing boy holds out his palms
Until they are white

YET DO I MARVEL

COUNTEE CULLEN

I doubt not God is good, well-meaning, kind,
And did He stoop to quibble could tell why
The little buried mole continues blind,
Why flesh that mirrors Him must some day die,
Make plain the reason tortured Tantalus
Is baited by the fickle fruit, declare
If merely brute caprice dooms Sisyphus
To struggle up a never-ending stair.
Inscrutable His ways are, and immune
To catechism by a mind too strewn
With petty cares to slightly understand
What awful brain compels His awful hand.
Yet do I marvel at this curious thing:
To make a poet black, and bid him sing!

THE TRAIN RUNS LATE TO HARLEM

Conrad Kent Rivers

Each known mile comes late.
Faces that leave with me earlier,
Return, sit and wait.
We made eight gruesome hours today.
And lunch; lunch we barely ate,
Watching today tick away.

One bravado is going to crash
One of those pine paneled suites
Where the boss sits, laying before
Him mankind's pleas. Old Boss
In his wild sophisticated way,
He'll quote from Socrates or Plato,
Then confess to be one of us.

I'll take Sunday's long way home,
Ride those waves;
Book passage around the world.
New house: boarding school for my
Kids, free rides at Riverside, buy
Out Sherman's barbecue,
Lift my people from poverty,
Until my train pops 133rd square
In her tiger's mouth
Returning me, returning me.

AWARD

....

*[A gold watch to the FBI man
who has followed me for 25 years.]*

RAY DUREM

Well, old spy
looks like I
led you down some pretty blind alleys,
took you on several trips to Mexico,
fishing in the high Sierras,
jazz at the Philharmonic.
You've watched me all your life,
I've clothed your wife,
put your two sons through college.
what good has it done?
sun keeps rising every morning.
Ever see me buy an Assistant President?
or close a school?
or lend money to Somoza?
I bought some after-hours whiskey in L.A.
but the Chief got his pay.
I ain't killed no Koreans,
or fourteen-year-old boys in Missisippi
neither did I bomb Guatemala,
or lend guns to shoot Algerians.
I admit I took a Negro child
to a white rest room in Texas,

but she was my daughter, only three,
and she had to pee,
and I just didn't know what to do,
would you?
see, I'm so light, it don't seem right
to go to the colored rest room;
my daughter's brown, and folks frown on that in Texas,
I just don't know how to go to the bathroom in the
   free world!

Now, old FBI man,
you've done the best you can,
you lost me a few jobs,
scared a couple landlords,
You got me struggling for that bread,
but I ain't dead.
and before it's all through,
I may be following you!

STATUS SYMBOL

MARI EVANS

i
Have Arrived

i
   am the
New Negro

   i
am the result of
President Lincoln
World War I
and Paris
the
Red Ball Express
white drinking fountains
sitdowns and
sit-ins
Federal Troops
Marches on Washington
   and
prayer meetings . . .

today
They hired me
it
is a status
job . . .
along
with my papers
They
gave me my
Status Symbol
the
key
to the
White . . . Locked . . .
John

BLACK IS
A SOUL

JOSEPH WHITE

Down
Down into the fathomless depths
Down into the abyss beneath the stone
Down still farther, to the very bottom
    of the infinite
Where black-eyed peas & greens are stored

Where de lawd sits among melon rinds.
A dark blue sound (funky & barefooted)
    entered & sang a tear for the People
Of black women (buxom & beautiful)
With nappy heads & cocoa filled breasts
    nippled with molasses,
    & their legs sensual & long beneath
    short bright dresses
& of black men greasy from the sun-soaked
    fields sitting in the shade,
    their guitars, the willow & the
    squatting sun weeping authentic blues

These quantums of pure soul
Who pick cotton under the rant rays of the sun
Who eat hot greasy fish, chitlins, corn pone,
    pig feet, fat back & drink wine
    on Sat. nights

Who get happy & swing tambourines & sing
    them there spirituals
Who are blessed by the power of poverty
Who bathe their feet in streamlets of
    simplicity
Who are torn by the insolence & depression
    of bigot blonde America,
Are the essence of beauty
The very earth
The good earth
The black earth

In these moments when my man preaches
    about a no good nigger woman who did
    him wrong
My fingers begin to pop
My feet jump alive
The blue sound clutches me to its bosom
    until I become that sound
In these moments when the sun is blue
When the rivers flow with wine
When the neck bone tree is in blossom
I raise my down bent kinky head to charlie
    & shout
I'm black. I'm black
& I'm from Look Back

JACKET NOTES

ISHMAEL REED

Being a colored poet
Is like going over
Niagara Falls in a
Barrel

An 8 year old can do what
You do unaided
The barrel maker doesn't
Think you can cut it

The gawkers on the bridge
Hope you fall on your
Face

The tourist bus full of
Paying customers broke-down
Just out of Buffalo

Some would rather dig
The postcards than
Catch your act

A mile from the brink
It begins to storm

But what really hurts is
You're bigger than the
Barrel

THE HOPE
OF YOUR UNBORN

THE STILL VOICE
OF HARLEM

CONRAD KENT RIVERS

Come to me broken dreams and all
    bring me the glory of fruitless souls,
I shall find a place for them in my gardens.

Weep not for the golden sun of California,
    think not of the fertile soil of Alabama . . .
nor your father's eyes, your mother's body
    twisted by the washing board.

I am the hope of your unborn,
    truly, when there is no more of me . . .
there shall be no more of you . . .

DREAM VARIATION

LANGSTON HUGHES

To fling my arms wide
In some place of the sun,
To whirl and to dance
Till the white day is done.
Then rest at cool evening
Beneath a tall tree
While night comes on gently,
    Dark like me —
That is my dream!

To fling my arms wide
In the face of the sun,
Dance! Whirl! Whirl!
Till the quick day is done.
Rest at pale evening . . .
A tall, slim tree . . .
Night coming tenderly
    Black like me.

LISTEN CHILDREN

LUCILLE CLIFTON

listen children
keep this in the place
you have for keeping
always
keep it all ways

we have never hated black

listen
we have been ashamed
hopeless   tired   mad
but always
all ways
we loved us

we have always loved each other
children   all ways

pass it on

change-up

HAKI MADHUBUTI

change-up,
let's go for ourselves
both cheeks are broken now.
change-up,
move past the corner bar,
let yr/split lift u above that quick high.
change-up,
that tooth pick you're sucking on was
once a log.
change-up,
and yr/children will look at u differently
than   we looked at our parents.

SUICIDE

ALICE WALKER

First, suicide notes should be
(not long) but written
second,
all suicide notes
should be signed
in blood
by hand
and to the point —
that point being, perhaps,
that there is none.
Thirdly, if it is the thought
of rest that
fascinates
laziness should be admitted
in the clearest terms.
Then, all things done
ask those outraged
consider their happiest
summer
& tell if the days it
adds up to
is one.

FOR EACH OF YOU

Audre Lorde

Be who you are and will be
learn to cherish
that boisterous Black Angel that drives you
up one day and down another
protecting the place where your power rises
running like hot blood
from the same source
as your pain.

When you are hungry
learn to eat
whatever sustains you
until morning
but do not be misled by details
simply because you live them.

Do not let your head deny
your hands
any memory of what passes through them
nor your eyes
nor your heart
everything can be used

except what is wasteful
(you will need
to remember this when you are accused of destruction.)
Even when they are dangerous
examine the heart of those machines you hate
before you discard them
and never mourn the lack of their power
lest you be condemned
to relive them.

If you do not learn to hate
you will never be lonely
enough
to love easily
nor will you always be brave
although it does not grow any easier.
Do not pretend to convenient beliefs
even when they are righteous
you will never be able to defend your city
while shouting.

Remember our sun
is not the most noteworthy star
only the nearest.

Respect whatever pain you bring back
from your dreaming
but do not look for new gods
in the sea
nor in any part of a rainbow.
Each time you love
love as deeply
as if it were
forever
only nothing is
eternal.

Speak proudly to your children
where ever you may find them
tell them
you are the offspring of slaves
and your mother was
a princess
in darkness.

THE MEN

E. ETHELBERT MILLER

What then shall we say to this?
If God is for us, who is against us?
    - Romans 8:31

I
Today I saw black men
carrying babies,
pushing carriages,
holding their own.

II
Our streets filled
with good news,
we must write the
headlines ourselves.

III
When the world
makes a fist
we duck and counterpunch,
we jab and swing.

IV
Black men
at construction sites
lifting black earth,
black hearts, black
hands.

V
The young men
dress in black,
their clothes
just big enough
for love.

POEMS FOR MY BROTHER KENNETH, VII

OWEN DODSON

Sleep late with your dream.
The morning has a scar
To mark on the horizon
With death of the morning star.

The color of blood will appear
And wash the morning sky,
Aluminum birds flying with fear
Will scream to your waking,
Will send you to die;

Sleep late with your dream.
Pretend that the morning is far,
Deep in the horizon country,
Unconcerned with the morning star.

IN TIME OF CRISIS

RAYMOND RICHARD PATTERSON

You are the brave who do not break
In the grip of the mob when the blow comes straight
To the shattered bone; when the sockets shriek;
When your arms lie twisted under your back.

Good men holding their courage slack
In their frightened pockets see how weak
The work that is done — and feel the weight
Of your blood on the ground for their spirits' sake;

And build their anger, stone on stone —
Each silently, but not alone.

THE NOONDAY APRIL SUN

GEORGE LOVE

when through the winding cobbled streets of time
new spring is borne upon the voices of young boys
when all around the grass grows up like laughter
and visions grow like grass beneath our feet
then roads run out like wine
and eyes like tongues drink up the streams of longing

o then remembrance rages at the tyranny of days
and men within their shabby inward rooms
get up to press their faces to the windowpanes
and then run down in rivers to the sea of dreams

AFTER THE WINTER

CLAUDE MCKAY

Some day, when trees have shed their leaves
   And against the morning's white
The shivering birds beneath the eaves
   Have sheltered for the night,
We'll turn our faces southward, love,
   Toward the summer isle
Where bamboos spire the shafted grove
   And wide-mouthed orchids smile.

And we will seek the quiet hill
   Where towers the cotton tree,
And leaps the laughing crystal rill,
   And works the droning bee.
And we will build a cottage there
   Beside an open glade,
With black-ribbed bluebells blowing near,
   And ferns that never fade.

FOUR SHEETS TO THE WIND AND A ONE-WAY TICKET TO FRANCE

Conrad Kent Rivers

As a child
I bought a red scarf and women told me
                              how beautiful it looked.
Wandering through the sous-sols as France
                              wandered through me.

In the evenings
I would watch the funny people make love
                              the way Maupassant said.
My youth allowed me the opportunity to hear
                              all those strange
verbs conjugated in erotic affirmations. I knew love at
    twelve.

When Selassie went before his peers and Dillinger
    goofed
I read in two languages, not really caring which one
                              belonged to me.

My mother lit a candle for George, my father
                              went broke, we died.

When I felt blue, the Champs understood, and when
                                        it was crowded
the alley behind Harry's New York Bar soothed
                                        my restless spirit.

I liked to watch the nonconformists gaze at the
    paintings
along Gauguin's bewildered paradise.

Braque once passed me in front of the Café Musique.
I used to watch those sneaky professors examine the
    populace.
Americans never quite fitted in, but they tried so we
    smiled.

I guess the money was too much for my folks.
Hitler was such a prig and a scare, we caught the long
    boat.
I stayed.

Main Street was never the same. I read Gide and tried
    to
translate Proust. Now nothing is real except French wine.
For absurdity is my reality, my loneliness unreal, my
    mind tired.

And I shall die an old Parisian.

FOR MY PEOPLE

Margaret Walker

For my people everywhere singing their slave songs
repeatedly: their dirges and their ditties and their
blues and jubilees, praying their prayers nightly
to an unknown god, bending their knees humbly
to an unseen power;

For my people lending their strength to the years, to
the gone years and the now years and the maybe
years, washing ironing cooking scrubbing sewing
mending hoeing plowing digging planting pruning
patching dragging along never gaining never reap-
ing never knowing and never understanding;

For my playmates in the clay and dust and sand of
Alabama backyards playing baptizing and preach-
ing and doctor and jail and soldier and school and
mama and cooking and playhouse and concert and
store and hair and Miss Choomby and company;

For the cramped bewildered years we went to school
to learn to know the reasons why and the answers
to and the people who and the places where and
the days when, in memory of the bitter hours
when we discovered we were black and poor and
small and different and nobody cared and nobody
wondered and nobody understood;

For the boys and girls who grew in spite of these things
to be man and woman, to laugh and dance and
sing and play and drink their wine and religion
and success, to marry their playmates and bear
children and then die of consumption and anemia
and lynching;

For my people thronging 47th Street in Chicago and
Lenox Avenue in New York and Rampart Street
in New Orleans, lost disinherited dispossessed and
happy people filling the cabarets and taverns and
other people's pockets needing bread and shoes
and milk and land and money and something —
something all our own;

For my people walking blindly spreading joy, losing
time being lazy, sleeping when hungry, shouting
when burdened, drinking when hopeless, tied and
shackled and tangled among ourselves by the
unseen creatures who tower over us omnisciently
and laugh;

For my people blundering and groping and floundering
in the dark of churches and schools and clubs
and societies, associations and councils and com-
mittees and conventions, distressed and disturbed
and deceived and devoured by money-hungry
glory-craving leeches, preyed on by facile force of
state and fad and novelty, by false prophet and
holy believer;

For my people standing staring trying to fashion a
betterway from confusion, from hypocrisy and
misunder-standing, trying to fashion a world that
will hold all the people, all the faces, all the adams
and eves and their countless generations;

Let a new earth rise. Let another world be born. Let a bloody peace be written in the sky. Let a second generation full of courage issue forth; let a people loving freedom come to growth. Let a beauty full of healing and a strength of final clenching be the pulsing in our spirits and our blood. Let the martial songs be written, let the dirges disappear. Let a race of men now rise and take control.

Afterword
THIRTY YEARS AFTER WORDS

I add these personal words with great pride and true celebration. This anthology was my first publication, in 1968, a product of my personal and teaching lives, a natural production of its times. *I Am the Darker Brother* has remained in print all of these almost thirty years, becoming a part of several generations of young readers and their older allies.

As teacher and poet, I wanted to present to my students, of all racial and ethnic backgrounds, the complete vision of *an* American literature. I was driven by the need to include some parts of the omitted: the powerful and varied creations and voices of African American poets. I wanted to add, to construct and reconstruct a true picture of an inclusive literature . . . to validate the very concept of an "American" poetry for us all.

I remember well, for the first edition, digging through shelves of used book and magazine stores, ransacking libraries, following poet trails through generations of literary and racial undergrounds. I remember walking into Manhattan editorial offices, both arms weighed with double-bagged shopping bags full of Black poetry . . . dumping books and pamphlets and piles of xeroxed poems on some neat executive desk . . . attempting to build a house of poetic truth with piles of paper.

I was proud to place this anthology in a long line of African American poetry collections, created by William Stanley Braithwaite, Countee Cullen, Arna Bontemps, Langston Hughes, and Clarence Major. Thirty years later, I can direct readers to fine anthologies by Robert Hayden, Dudley Randall, Sonia Sanchez, Gwendolyn Brooks, E. Ethelbert Miller, and Michael S. Harper, among others. Clarence Major has edited *The Garden Thrives,* the first comprehensive twentieth-century collection since my own *The Poetry of Black America.*

And I can continue to direct readers from *I Am The Darker Brother* to other anthologies, old and new, in bookstores and in libraries. Seek out the small presses, the literary magazines, the local workshops and readings. We need to listen to the poets who rap and rant—with music and without—and perform in public places, publishing their poems into the air first, before publishing onto the printed page.

The work is too rich for a single presentation, a single form. The work is too rich for the limits of a single book. The craft and force of African American poets of this century could never be presented in a single collection, even if there were no limits applied by any publisher. When I began to reread and select the various "must have" poets and poems that appeared after the mid-1960s, I amassed a true "second anthology" of ninety poets, over 200 poems. Eventually, only ten percent of the "must haves" could be included in this edition.

The extraordinary literary line of the body of work continues. The celebration continues. With the republication of this anthology, expanded to include nineteen new poets not represented in the first edition, this longed-for true picture of an inclusive American literature continues to form and shape and color with the depth of its parallel lines of people and poetry. These shaped shouts and groans, the laughs and accusatory screams, continue to add their reverberations to the "joyful noise" of an expanding chorus of affirmation. These poems give words and music to the drama of our developing lives, to the drama of our developing country. Full spotlight. Center stage. Impossible to be ignored. Silence nevermore.

Nearly thirty years after its original publication, I present, again, this anthology of African American poetry. The original collection of poems remains intact. Twenty-one new poems have been added, as have contributions by Rudine Sims Bishop and Nikki Giovanni, both introducing this new edition. Finally, as editor of this anthology, I have moved my own word to the back of the book . . . hoping, once again, to teach by example.

We are, all of us, part of this "parallel-culture" country, beyond race and gender, generation and geography. African American young people must continue their struggles to resurrect the strong literary heritage that is the foundation of any survival, must continue to discover their modern-times "practicing-poets," and wear their words like armor as they grow proud lives. And all of us, from all the colors of the race, must share in this continuing literature. We can share these visions, and join with these African American voices, to share the equality of strength that must be common language for all of our American lives. Together.

ARNOLD ADOFF

Notes

ME AND THE MULE *LANGSTON HUGHES*

For over a century, "Black" was a term used to describe "Negroes" as inferiors or underlings. But with the coming of a vigorous civil rights movement and the gaining of independence by African nations, the negative use of "Black" has diminished considerably. African Americans began using this simple and direct word themselves with a great amount of pride, in such phrases as "I'm a Black man" or "I'm a Black American," and with a sense of racial identification with Black peoples all over the world.

THE NEGRO SPEAKS OF RIVERS
LANGSTON HUGHES

W. E. B. DuBois (1868-1963) was an important figure in African American life. He was a professor of economics, history, and sociology, and the author of many books, one of the best known of which is *The Souls of Black Folk* (1903). Mr. DuBois was a founder of the National Association for the Advancement of Colored People, and editor of its magazine, *Crisis,* in which this poem first appeared.

O DAEDALUS, FLY AWAY HOME *ROBERT HAYDEN*

Daedalus was a character in Greek mythology who built wings for himself and for his son, Icarus, with which they were able to fly.

Juba, a dance developed by Southern slaves, is also the name of a thousand-mile river flowing from Southern Ethiopia to the Indian Ocean.

Juju and conjo are African fetish objects having mystical powers, used in rituals.

DUST BOWL *ROBERT A. DAVIS*

During the 1920's and through the years of the Great Depression, the rich topsoil of the once fertile lands of the Southwestern United States was blown away, leaving vast areas of dusty plain. Thousands of Americans who had settled and farmed this land were forced to migrate to usually inhospitable and poorer areas in other states.

A BALLAD OF REMEMBRANCE *ROBERT HAYDEN*

The dictionary meaning of quadroon is "one who is one-fourth Negro, the offspring of a mulatto and a white." With our modern knowledge of the inability of scientists to find exact proportions of "Negro" and "white" in a person, we know this definition is misleading. Here the word indicates racially mixed origins.

Mark Van Doren was an American poet and teacher of great renown.

MIDDLE PASSAGE   *ROBERT HAYDEN*

Mongo is an ethnic and linguistic division of Bantu tribes living south of the great bend of the Congo River.

Barracoons are enclosures or barracks built and used for the temporary confinement of slaves.

Conjo are African fetish objects having mystical powers, used in rituals.

Fellatah (Fellata) are Egyptian and Sudanese "Negro" peoples.

Ibo is one of a group of "Negro" tribes living on the Lower Niger River. American slaves from this region were called Eboe.

Kru is one tribe of Black peoples from the Liberian region of Africa.

Mandingo are Black tribes living in the Western Sudan.

The final section of this epic poem follows accounts of the *Amistad* mutiny of 1839. During their shipment as slaves in the *Amistad,* a Spanish ship, the African captives mutinied. The mutiny was successful, but the ship was steered to the United States waters by one of its crew, instead of to Africa. The men were brought to New London, Connecticut, placed on trial, and defended by John Quincy Adams. The case went to the United States Supreme Court which, in a historic decision, upheld the lower court's decision, and freed the mutineers. They were allowed to return to Africa in 1841.

FREDERICK DOUGLASS *ROBERT HAYDEN*

Frederick Douglass was born a slave. He escaped to freedom from Baltimore in 1838 and began a career as an abolitionist, writer, and orator. Working as a laborer, Douglass attended antislavery society meetings and conventions in Massachusetts, where his speeches were so eloquent that he became a lecturer for the Massachusetts Anti-Slavery Society.

Douglass escaped to England in 1845 to avoid reenslavement, but was able to return and buy his freedom. He established an abolitionist newspaper, was active as a lecturer, and supported education for Blacks, and the cause for women's suffrage in this country.

He was an advisor to John Brown, and after Brown was arrested, following the 1859 raid on Harpers Ferry, Douglass had to leave America again, going first to Canada, and then to England. During the Civil War he was very active in raising regiments of Black soldiers for the North, and he was constantly agitated for civil rights and suffrage for African Americans.

His autobiography, *Life and Times of Frederick Douglass,* is a well-written and still moving account of Southern slave life, as well as the personal story of a great writer and intellect.

In 1889, his appointment as Consul-General to Haiti gave him some measure of national recognition for a life spent in service to his people and country.

His writings have provided a philosophical basis for programs aimed at social and economic equality, both in his own time and today.

Runagate Runagate *ROBERT HAYDEN*

The word "runagate" is a variation on "renegade," and means a wanderer, fugitive, or runaway.

Over one hundred thousand slaves escaped from the South between 1810 and 1850, running, walking, riding from station to station on the Underground Railroad. There were over three thousand active men and women, mostly Black, who worked independently to help the escapees along this journey. These were the "conductors" on the "railroad," which was actually a secret network of houses, churches, inns, stores, and trails to help fugitive slaves in their flight to the North. This system is known to have existed as early as 1786, but without benefit of formal organization.

Among the thousands who guided escaping slaves to freedom was Harriet Tubman. Born about 1821, an ex-slave herself, she was known as "Moses" and "The General." She made many trips back into the Southern states, at great personal risk, to lead her family and other slaves to the North. Called "Stealer of Slaves" by the owners, she had a price on her head, and was a hunted woman who could have been shot on sight.

Until her death, Harriet Tubman was a world-renowned and eloquent voice for full freedom for African Americans.

William Lloyd Garrison, Bronson Alcott, Ralph
Waldo Emerson, Thomas Garrett, Frederick Douglass,
Henry David Thoreau, and John Brown were all opposed
to slavery in their writings and actions.

MEMORIAL WREATH   *DUDLEY RANDALL*

Toussaint L'Ouverture (1743-1803) was a military and
political leader and one of the liberators of Haiti.

A POEM FOR BLACK HEARTS   *AMIRI BARAKA*

Malcolm X was a leader in the Nation of Islam religion
and shortly before his death he organized his own politi-
cal and civil rights group. His assassination, while he
was speaking at a meeting in New York's Audubon
Ballroom, cut short his development as a leader of
African American thought and action.

Malcolm X was criticized severely during his first
few years of activity, by both the American mass media
and some Black leaders. Ironically, since his death and
the publication of *The Autobiography of Malcolm X,* his
racial views and programs for achieving economic and
political parity have been given credence by many
African Americans. Malcolm X spoke above all else for
dignity for the Black man.

Amiri Baraka wrote this poem soon after Malcolm
X's death in February, 1965.

VATICIDE   *MYRON O'HIGGINS*

Mohandas Gandhi, a leader of the people of India until

his assassination in 1948, fought for the independence of his nation and for various political and social programs through the use of his nonviolent demonstrations, hunger fasts, and civil disobedience.

Gandhi's writings and actions strongly influenced the Reverend Martin Luther King and other leaders of the nonviolent civil rights movement in America.

This poem was written in 1948, during the week following Gandhi's death.

YARDBIRD'S SKULL   *OWEN DODSON*

Charlie Parker was a jazz alto saxophone player who was an innovator in improvisation and in his approach to this truly American music. He inspired a generation of musicians and listeners. After his death there grew around his memory a legend exemplified in the slogan, "Bird Lives."

MONTGOMERY   *SAM CORNISH*

On December 1, 1955, Mrs. Rosa Parks refused to "move to the rear" of the Cleveland Avenue bus in Montgomery, Alabama, as required by the rule of racial segregation of that time. Her arrest was the spark that ignited the 382-day-long Montgomery bus boycott, the protest movement that thrust the techniques of non-violence, and the leadership of Dr. Martin Luther King into the forefront of the American consciousness, and was one of the beginnings of the African American Civil Rights movement of the 1950's and 1960's.

Here Where Coltrane Is *MICHAEL S. HARPER*

John Coltrane was one of the most influential creators of a new jazz music during the 1950's, until his untimely death in 1967. He was an extraordinary soloist on saxophone, as well as an innovative force in the development of a "free-form" jazz, evolving from the musical and social realities of that time. His "teachings" have continued to grow in stature, during the last decades; his horn a particular source of inspiration to a generation of poets.

Martin Luther King Jr. *GWENDOLYN BROOKS*

Martin Luther King Jr. was a dynamic figure in twentieth century world history, until his assassination in 1968. Dr. King was the major leader of the civil rights movement in this country from the mid-1950's, and, at the time of his death, was broadening his efforts in the struggles for economic and social equalities for poor peoples everywhere.

If We Must Die *CLAUDE McKAY*

When Winston Churchill, the Prime Minister of England, addressed a joint session of the United States Congress in 1941, he quoted the final lines of this poem to urge the United States to join with Europe against the German attack.

Tired *FENTON JOHNSON*

Fenton Johnson was one of the first of the African

American "revolutionary" poets. He broke away from the conventional approach of early twentieth-century "Negro" poetry, with its use of dialect and traditional literary form. His poems, as here shown in "Tired," are for the most part in free verse and natural speech patterns, and they echo the disillusionment Black Americans were experiencing during the 1920's.

James Weldon Johnson wrote of Fenton Johnson's poetry in 1931: "He went further than protests against wrong or the moral challenge that the wronged can always fling against the wrongdoer; *he sounded the note of fatalistic despair.*"

AWARD *RAY DUREM*

Members of the Somoza family had controlled Nicaragua since 1936, when General Anastasio Somoza seized power, until their overthrow in 1979.

The Assistant President referred to is Sherman Adams.

YET DO I MARVEL *COUNTEE CULLEN*

Tantalus was a character in Greek mythology who was punished for revealing the secrets of the gods to men. He was condemned to an eternity of standing, hungry and thirsty, in water up to his chin, beneath a tree laden with fruit. Whenever he tried to eat or drink, the water and fruit receded.

Sisyphus was a king of Corinth, in Greek mythology,

who was condemned in Hades to roll a heavy stone continually up a steep hill, only to have it roll down again each time he reached the top.

STATUS SYMBOL   *MARI EVANS*

The "Red Ball Express" was a World War II truck supply route that ran from the ports and beaches of Europe up to the front lines. Nearly all the drivers were Black.

FOUR SHEETS TO THE WIND AND A ONE
WAY TICKET TO FRANCE
CONRAD KENT RIVERS

The Champs Elysées is a famous boulevard on the right bank of Paris, known for its cafés, shops, and theaters.

Biographies

AI was born in Tucson, Arizona, in 1947, and attended the University of Arizona and the University of California at Irvine. She is the author of several collections of poetry, including *Cruelty*, *Sin*, *Fate*, and *Killing Floor*, which was a Lamont Poetry Award winner of the Academy of American poets.

SAMUEL ALLEN (PAUL VESEY) was born in Columbus, Ohio, in 1917. He studied with James Weldon Johnson at Fisk University, received an LL.D. from Harvard Law School, and later studied at the Sorbonne, in Paris. There, Richard Wright was helpful in securing publication of Mr. Allen's poems in *Présence Africaine*, a French magazine. Using the name Paul Vesey, Mr. Allen published his first book, *El fenbeinzaehne* (*Ivory Tusks*), in a bilingual edition in Germany. His poetry has since been printed in numerous magazines and anthologies in this country. He has traveled in Africa and in Latin America, and has been assistant General Counsel in the Legal Department of the United States Information Agency. Mr. Allen has worked with the Community Relations Service of the Department of Justice, a Federal civil rights agency attempting to facilitate peaceful racial integration. Recent publications include *Paul Vesey's Ledger* and *Every Round*. He is Professor Emeritus of English, Boston University.

MAYA ANGELOU was born in St. Louis in 1928. She has had a celebrated and varied career as an actress, director, producer, social activist, and spokesperson. Her prose books, *I Know Why the Caged Bird Sings* and *Gather Together in My Name* are perennial best-sellers. Among her poetry collections are *And I Still Rise* and *I Shall Not Be Moved*. She is currently teaching at Wake Forest University, Winston-Salem, North Carolina.

AMIRI BARAKA was born LeRoi Jones in Newark, New Jersey, in 1934. He studied at Howard and Columbia Universities and at the New School in New York City. He has been an editor of *Yugen* and *Kulchur* magazines, and has published his poetry extensively in many other periodicals, as well as being a writer on jazz for *Downbeat*, *Metronome*, and other publications. *Preface to a Twenty Volume Suicide Note* was his first book of poems, published in 1961. He is also the author of a book of poems entitled *The Dead Lecturer* (1964), and several plays which have been produced with much success in New York City. *Dutchman*, one of his plays, has been made into a motion picture. Among the seventeen collections of his poetry is *Selected Poetry of Amiri Baraka/LeRoi Jones*. He is a professor at the State University of New York at Stony Brook.

ARNA BONTEMPS was born in Alexandria, Louisiana, in 1902,

and was educated at Pacific Union College and at the University of Chicago. His poetry appeared in magazines between 1924 and 1931, and won many awards and critical recognition. He has written prose books, is the author of a number of books for children, and was coeditor, with Langston Hughes, of *The Poetry of the Negro: 1746-1949*, an anthology. Mr. Bontemps was the librarian at Fisk University for many years. His poetry was collected in a 1963 publication, *Personals*. He died in 1973.

GWENDOLYN BROOKS was born in Topeka, Kansas, and was educated in Chicago, where she has lived almost her entire life. *A Street in Bronzeville*, published in 1945, was her first book of poems. It was followed by *Annie Allen*, which won the Pulitzer Prize for poetry in 1950. Other books of her poems are *The Bean Eaters* and *Selected Poems*. s. Brooks is also the author of a novel, *Maude Martha*, and books of verse for children. Recent books include *Blacks*, and an autobiography, *Report from Part One*. She is the author of thirty books, and the recipient of over seventy honorary degrees and awards, including her appointment as Poet Laureate of Illinois.

STERLING A. BROWN was born in 1901 in Washington, D.C., and was educated in that city's schools, as well as at Williams College and Harvard University. He had a long and distinguished career at Howard University, where he held a professorship in English, and was selected to write a history of the University in 1961. His books include *Southern Road*, a volume of his poetry published in 1932, *The Negro in American Fiction* (1938), and *Negro Poetry and Drama* (1938). Mr. Brown was senior editor of the well-known anthology, *Negro Caravan*, and author of other volumes, including *The Collected Poems of Sterling A. Brown*. Mr. Brown died in 1989.

LUCILLE CLIFTON was born in Depew, New York, in 1936. She is Distinguished Professor of Humanities at St. Mary's College of Maryland, and the author of more than thirty collections of poetry for adults and children. Among her publications are *Good Times*, *Good News About the Earth*, and a series of seminal books for young readers, the *Everett Anderson* books.

SAM CORNISH was born in Baltimore in 1935. His collections of poetry include *Your Hand in Mine*, for young audiences, *Generations*, *Sam's World*, and *Folks Like Me* He makes his home in Boston, Massachussetts, where he teaches at Emerson College.

COUNTEE CULLEN was born in 1903 in New York City, and was educated in the city's public schools and at New York University. He received his master's degree from Harvard and became a teacher in New York City, a career he continued all his life. When he was twenty-two years old his first book of poems, *Color*, was published and won the Harmon Gold Award for Literature. His other books include *Copper Sun* (1927), *The Black Christ* (1929), *The Medea and Other Poems* (1935), and *The Lost Zoo* (1940). *On These I Stand*, published posthumously in 1947, is a volume of selected poems. Since his untimely death in 1946, Countee Cullen's reputation as a lyric poet has steadily grown.

FRANK MARSHALL DAVIS was born in Arkansas City, Kansas, in 1905. He was educated at Kansas State College and then began a career in journalism. He helped to establish the

Atlanta Daily World, and later became executive editor of the *Associated Negro Press* in Chicago. He has been a Rosenwald Fellow in poetry, and has published three books of his poems: *Black Man's Verse* (1935), *I Am the American Negro* (1937), and *47th Street* (1948). Mr. Davis died in 1987.

ROBERT A. DAVIS was born in Mobile, Alabama, in 1917. He attended high school in Chicago, and the University of Chicago and Chicago Christian Junior College. He has contributed to magazines, and has been active in theater production in the Chicago area.

TOI DERRICOTTE was born in Detroit in 1941. She is the recipient of a National Endowment for the Arts Fellowship, and her work has been widely published. Her collections of poetry include *Captivity, Natural Birth,* and *The Empress of the Death House.* She teaches at Old Dominion University, in Virginia.

OWEN DODSON was born in 1914 in Brooklyn, and was educated in the public schools of that borough and at Bates College. He received a Master of Fine Arts degree at Yale, where two of his plays were produced. Several of his other plays have been produced at various colleges. Mr. Dodson was head of the Department of Drama at Howard University, in Washington, D.C. *Powerful Long Ladder* and *Come Home Early, Child* are among his publications. He died in 1983.

RITA DOVE was born in Akron in 1952. She is the author of eight collections of poetry, including *Grace Notes* and *Selected Poems.* Among her awards and honors is a 1987 Pulitzer Prize, and the appointment for two terms as the Poet Laureate of the United States.

PAUL LAURENCE DUNBAR was born in Dayton in 1872, the son of former slaves—his father had escaped by way of the Underground Railroad. He was unable to attend college, and went to work as an elevator operator. He was holding this job when his first volume of poems, *Oak and Ivy*, appeared in 1893. *Majors and Minors* followed in 1895. They paved the way for the great success of Dunbar's *Lyrics of a Lowly Life*, published in 1896. This book gave Dunbar a national reputation, the first time in 125 years—since Phyllis Wheatley—that an African American poet had received such wide recognition. Dunbar continued to write much poetry and prose, though suffering from tuberculosis; the illness caused his early death in 1906. His *Complete Poems* was published in 1913, and heralded the new era in literature that began in the early twentieth century for African Americans.

RAY DUREM was born in Seattle in 1915. He joined the U.S. Navy at fourteen, and later fought as a member of the International Brigades during the Spanish Civil War. He lived for many years in Mexico, but returned to the United States for medical treatment. He died in Los Angeles, California, in December, 1963, prior to the publication of many of his poems. His work has appeared in the magazines *Umbra* and *Negro Digest*, as well as in many anthologies bothhere and in Europe. A collection of his poetry, *Take No Prisoners*, was published in 1972.

MARI EVANS was born and educated in Toledo and now makes her home in Indianapolis. She has been a songwriter, civil-service employee, and choir director, and plays both piano and organ. She publishes in numerous magazines, and is active at writers' conferences. She is a producer, director, and author of plays, fiction, and screenplays. She has taught at Indiana University, Cornell, the University of Miami, and Spellman College in Atlanta. Poetry collections include *Where Is All the Music?*, *I Am a Black Woman*, *Whisper*, and *A Dark and Splendid Mass*.

NIKKI GIOVANNI was born in Knoxville, Tennessee, in 1943. She has published more than twenty books of poetry and essays, and is one of the most visible American poets. Travelling and speaking around the country, she has become known for her political and social commentary, as well as her poetic podium style. Some of her published works include *Spin a Soft Black Song*, *Ego Tripping and Other Poems for Young Readers*, *The Women and the Men*, *My House*, *Racism 101*, and *Sacred Cows . . . and Other Edibles*. She is a professor of English at Virginia Polytechnic Institute in Blacksburg, Virginia.

MICHAEL S. HARPER was born in Brooklyn in 1938. He was raised in Los Angeles, and received degrees from California State University and the University of Iowa. Some of his poetry collections include *Dear John, Dear Coltrane*; *History Is Your Own Heartbeat*; and *Images of Kin: New and Selected Poems*. He resides in Providence, Rhode Island, where he is University Professor at Brown University. Among his many honors is his appointment as Poet Laureate of Rhode Island.

ROBERT HAYDEN was born in 1913 in Detroit, attended Wayne State University in that city, and then held a teaching assistantship at the University of Michigan. He received Hopwood awards for poetry on two occasions, and won fellowships from the Rosenwald and Ford Foundations. He published *Heartshape in the Dust*; *The Lion and the Archer*, a joint publication with Myron O'Higgins of their poetry; and *A Ballad of Remembrance*. *A Ballad of Remembrance* won first prize at the International Festival of Negro Arts held in 1966 in Dakar, Senegal. His *Selected Poems* was published in 1966. His poetry has appeared in *The Atlantic Monthly*, *Poetry*, *Negro Digest*, and other publications and anthologies. He joined the faculty of Fisk University in 1946 and was a professor of English there for twenty-two years. In 1975 he was elected a fellow of the American Academy of Poets, and in 1976 he became the first African American to be appointed poetry consultant to the Library of Congress. He was the author of nine collections of poetry, including *Angle of Ascent: New and Selected Poems*. He taught at the University of Michigan until his death in 1980. His *Collected Poems* was published in 1985.

CALVIN C. HERNTON was born in Chattanooga in 1934, and studied at Talladega College and Fisk University. Since 1970, he has been a professor at Oberlin College in Ohio. A writer of fiction and plays as well as poetry, Mr. Hernton has also been an editor of *Umbra* magazine, which he helped to found. He has published extensively in the field of sociology, including the landmark book, *Sex and Racism in America*. His poetry collections include *The Coming of the Chronos to the House of Nightsong* and *Medicine Man: Collected Poems*.

LESLIE PINCKNEY HILL was born in 1880 in Lynchburg, Virginia, where he was educated. He attended Harvard University, taught at Tuskegee Institute, and later became the principal of the Cheyney Training School for Teachers in Pennsylvania. His published works include *The Wings of Oppression* and *Toussaint L'Ouverture-A Dramatic History*. Mr. Hill died in 1960.

LANGSTON HUGHES was born in Joplin, Missouri, in 1902, and went to school in Lawrence, Kansas, and Cleveland, Ohio. He attended Columbia University, worked at odd jobs, shipped on freighters to Africa and Europe, and returned to study at Lincoln University in Pennsylvania, from which he graduated in 1929. He received many awards and honors, crossed the country on numerous occasions to give public readings of his poetry, and was a prolific writer for over forty years. He wrote novels, books of short stories, plays, newspaper columns, books for children, history books, and volumes of poetry, beginning with *The Weary Blues*, in 1926. His *Selected Poems* and *The Langston Hughes Reader* both appeared in 1958. Mr. Hughes made his home in New York City and was active in helping young writers who sought his advice and personal warmth. *Panther and the Lash*, a collection of his poetry, was published soon after his death in 1967.

LANCE JEFFERS was born in Fremont, Nebraska, in 1919. His poetry was widely anthologized during the 1960's and his collections, *My Blackness Is the Beauty of This Land* and *When I Know the Power of My Black Hand*, were influential to an emerging generation of African American poets. He was a professor of English at North Carolina State University and continued to publish poetry and articles until his death in 1985. His other collections of poetry include *O Africa, Where I Baked My Bread* and *Grandshire*.

FENTON JOHNSON was born in 1888 in Chicago, and was educated in that city. He attended the University of Chicago and produced original plays at the old Pekin Theatre on South State Street. He also edited and published several "little" literary magazines. *A Little Dreaming*, published in 1914, was his first volume of poetry. It was followed by *Visions of the Dusk* and *Songs of the Soil*. He published a book of short stories, *Tales of Darkest America*, in 1920. Mr. Johnson died in 1958.

JAMES WELDON JOHNSON was born in 1871 in Jacksonville, Florida, was educated there, and then attended Atlanta University. He had distinguished careers as a public school principal, lawyer, diplomat, executive secretary of the N.A.A.C.P., and professor of literature at Fisk University. He and his brother were the authors of "Lift Every Voice and Sing," a song that has become the "anthem" of African Americans. Johnson also wrote lyrics for musical shows and hit songs. Among his many published works are: *Fifty Years and Other Poems* (1917), *God's Trombones* (1927), *St. Peter Relates an Incident* (1930), and his autobiography, *Along This Way* (1933). He edited *The Book of American Negro Poetry*, first issued in 1922. Mr. Johnson died in an automobile accident in 1938.

ETHERIDGE KNIGHT was born in Corinth, Mississippi, in 1931. He was severely wounded during the Korean War, and eventually convicted for armed robbery. He educated himself in prison and started writing poetry, publishing *Poems From Prison* while still an inmate. Other collections of his work include *Belly Song* and *The Essential Etheridge Knight*. Mr. Knight died in 1991.

AUDRE LORDE was born in New York City in 1934. She was a teacher and librarian, recipient of many honors and awards, and professor of English at Hunter College. Her social activism and political insights were as inspirational as her poetry. Some of her collections of poems include *The First Cities*, *Cables To Rage*, *New York Head Shop and Museum*, *Coal*, and *Undersong: Chosen Poems Old and New*. Ms. Lorde died in 1992.

GEORGE LOVE was born in Charlotte, North Carolina. He graduated from Morehouse College in Atlanta, worked for the United States Government in Indonesia, and travelled widely in South America and Europe. His poems have been published in *New Negro Poets*, a collection edited by Langston Hughes. Mr. Love is also an art photographer and has exhibited his work in New York galleries.

CLAUDE MCKAY was born in Jamaica, the British West Indies, in 1891, but came to America in his early twenties to study at Tuskegee Institute in Alabama, and then at Kansas State University. He was involved in the literary life in New York City during the 1920s, and was an associate editor of the *Liberator*, under Max Eastman. *Harlem Shadows*, a book of poems published in 1922, was widely acclaimed. McKay spent almost ten years living abroad and published much prose, including *Home to Harlem* (1928), *Banjo* (1929), and *A Long Way from Home* (1937). He died in 1948, and his *Selected Poems* was published posthumously in 1953.

HAKI MADHUBUTI was born Don L. Lee in Little Rock, Arkansas, in 1942. He is a social critic, activist, and founding publisher of Third World Press. He is the author of *Black Pride*; *Don't Cry, Scream*; *We Walk the Way of the New World*; and *Directionscore: Selected and New Poems*, among other publications.

E. ETHELBERT MILLER was born in New York City in 1950. He is a graduate of Howard University, and is director of its African American Resource Center. Among his publications are an anthology of African American poetry, *In Search of Color Everywhere*, and collections of his own poetry, including *First Light: New and Selected Poems*.

MYRON O'HIGGINS was born in 1918. He was a student of Sterling A. Brown at Howard University, received Julius Rosenberg and Lucy Moten Fellowships, and studied and traveled widely abroad. His poems have been published in *The Lion and the Archer*, a collection he and Robert Hayden issued privately in 1948, and in many magazines and anthologies. He received a graduate degree at Yale, has been on the staff of the Museum of Primitive Art in New York City, and authored several experimental plays.

RAYMOND RICHARD PATTERSON was born in 1929 in New York City. He received his education at Lincoln University in Pennsylvania and at New York University. His poems have appeared in two British anthologies, *Sixes and Sevens* and *Beyond the Blues*, as well as in collections and magazines in this country. He is the author of short stories and a novel, and has been a professor of English at the City College of New York for more than twenty-five years. Some of his publications include *26 Ways of Looking at a Black Man* and *Elemental Blues*.

QUANDRA PRETTYMAN was born in Baltimore. She graduated from Antioch College and held a teaching fellowship at the University of Michigan, where she did graduate work. Ms. Prettyman has been a lecturer at the New School in New York City and a faculty member of the New York College of Insurance and the Summer Program at Connecticut College. She is married and lives in New York City, where she is a professor of English at Barnard College.

DUDLEY RANDALL was born in Washington, D.C., in 1914. He graduated from Wayne University in Detroit, received his master's degree in library science from the University of Michigan, and has been librarian of Lincoln University in Missouri and of Morgan College in Baltimore. He makes his home in Detroit and is associated with the Wayne County Public Library. Mr. Randall's poetry has appeared in *Midwest Journal*, *Umbra,* and *Free Lance*, as well as in many anthologies. He published *Poem Counterpoem*, in collaboration with Margaret Danner. Mr. Randall also runs the Broadside Press in Detroit, a company devoted to the publication of poetry by African Americans. He is the author of the influential anthologies *Black Poetry* and *The Black Poets*. His publications include *Cities Burning, More To*

Remember, and *A Litany of Friends: Poems Selected and New*.

ISHMAEL REED was born in Chattanooga in 1938. One of the most influential African American authors of our time, he has published more than twenty books of fiction and poetry. His publications include the novels *The Free-Lance Pallbearers*, *Yellow Back Radio Broke-Down*, and *Mumbo Jumbo*; collections of poetry include *Selected Poems*, *Conjure*, and *New and Collected Poems*. He teaches at the University of California at Berkeley.

CONRAD KENT RIVERS was born in Atlantic City in 1933. He graduated from Wilberforce University and did graduate work at Indiana University and the Chicago Teachers' College. He has been published in the *Kenyon Review*, *Antioch Review*, and *Negro Digest*, as well as in other magazines and in anthologies. A booklet of poems, *Perchance to Dream, Othello*, appeared in 1959. *These Black Bodies and This Sunburnt Face* was published in 1962. He published two more collections of his poetry, *Dusk at Selma* and *The Still Voice of Harlem* before his untimely death in 1968.

PRIMUS ST. JOHN was born in New York City in 1939. He has been a professor at Portland State University for more than twenty years, and has been the recipient of many honors and awards. Among his collections of poetry are *From Here We Speak* and *Love Is Not a Consolation; It Is a Light*.

SONIA SANCHEZ was born in Birmingham, Alabama, in 1935. She is an author of plays, stories, and widely-anthologized poetry. Her collections include *Homecoming*, *Poems for Young*

Brothas and Sistuhs, and *Homegirls and Handgrenades*. She has been a professor at Temple University, in Philadelphia, since 1977.

JEAN TOOMER was born in Washington, D.C., in 1894, and was educated at the University of Wisconsin and the College of the City of New York. His poems, short stories, and plays were published in the 1920s and received much praise from Sherwood Anderson, Hart Crane, and others. His work was collected in *Cane*, published in 1923. He died in 1967.

QUINCY TROUPE was born in 1943 in New York City, but was raised in Los Angeles, where he became a member of the celebrated Watts Writers' Workshop. He is the author of several prose books, including *Miles: The Autobiography*. He is the recipient of two American Book Awards and a Peabody Award for the Miles Davis Radio project. His collections of poetry include *Weather Reports: New and Selected Poems* and *Avalanche*. He teaches creative writing at the University of California at San Diego.

ALICE WALKER was born in Eatonton, Georgia, in 1944. She is the author of ten books of fiction, several collections of essays, and six volumes of poetry. Some of her publications include the novels *The Third Life of Grange Copeland* and *The Color Purple,* and *Revolutionary Petunias and Other Poems* and *Her Blue Body Everything We Know: Earthling Poems, 1965–1990*.

MARGARET WALKER was born in Birmingham, Alabama. She received a Master of Arts degree from the University of Iowa, and has been on the faculty of Jackson State College in Jackson, Mississippi, for many years. Her first book of poems,

For My People, won the Yale University Younger Poets competition, and was published in 1942. She has also received a Rosenwald Fellowship and has been a visiting lecturer at many colleges. Her first novel, *Jubilee* (1966), won a Houghton-Mifflin Literary Fellowship. Other collections of her poetry include *Prophets of a New Day*, *October Journey*, and *This Is My Century: New and Collected Poems*.

JOSEPH WHITE was born in Philadelphia but resides in New York City when he is not pursuing his travels and study. He has been published in the magazine *Dasein*; in *Burning Spear* (1963), a collection of poetry by African Americans; and in *Poets of Today*, and anthology of modern poetry.

RICHARD WRIGHT was born on a plantation near Natchez, Mississippi, in 1908. He was, for the most part, self-educated, and worked at many jobs until the publication of his first book, *Uncle Tom's Children*, in 1938. He received a Guggenheim Fellowship and published his first novel, *Native Son*, in 1940. It was a national sensation, and this success was followed five years later with an autobiography, *Black Boy*. Wright continued to publish while living in New York, but then moved with his family to France and remained an expatriate until his death in 1960.

AL YOUNG was born in Ocean Springs, Mississippi, in 1939, and grew up in Detroit. He has published five novels, edited anthologies, and authored three memoirs. Among his six collections of poetry is *Heaven: Collected Poems*. He has lived for many years in Palo Alto, California.

Index to Authors

Index to First Lines